THE PRIVATE EYE ANNUAL 2008

EDITED BY IAN HISLOP

Published in Great Britain by
Private Eye Productions Ltd
6 Carlisle Street, London W1D 5BN
www.private-eye.co.uk

© 2008 Pressdram Ltd
ISBN 1 901784 48 0
Designed by Bridget Tisdall
Printed and bound by
MPG Books Limited, Cornwall
2 4 6 8 10 9 7 5 3 1

THE PRIVATE EYE ANNUAL 2008

EDITED BY IAN HISLOP

McLACHLAN

"Could we borrow a cup of money?"

A Message From Northern Gnome

MAY I take this opportunity to assure savers and investors in Northern Gnome that my money is completely safe and that there is absolutely no need for me to panic.

There is no chance, I repeat no chance, of me losing a single penny of my considerable salary and bonus.

I hope that this firm statement will reassure my wife, Lady Gnome, who in recent days has taken to queuing outside my office seeking to withdraw large amounts of cash to spend on jewellery and other so-called "crisis proof financial accessories".

Let me reiterate to her and to others like her who may be concerned at this time that the Chancellor of the Exchequer has personally assured me that however abysmally I have run Northern Gnome he will guarantee huge sums of taxpayers money to enable me and my lady wife to live in a style to which we have long been accustomed. I thank you for your support and understanding.

Lord Gnome,
Northern Crock, New Newcastle,
The Cayman Islands.

We're Opeless
(surely "Open"? Ed)

NATIONALISATION LATEST

This Northern Rock business could make us look very silly

THE DEATH OF BECKET

Those 94 Questions Everyone Will Have To Answer Before They Are Allowed To Enter Or Leave Britain

1 What's your name?

2 Is that your real name?

3 Where do you live?

4 What is your sexual orientation?

5 Describe your ethnicity. Are you:
a) Black-Caucasian;
b) Oriental-Jewish;
c) Welsh;
d) Don't know;
e) Jedi Warrior.

6 What have you got in that bag?

7 Are you contemplating engaging in acts of terrorism during your stay?

8 Did you pack that bomb yourself?

9 Have you recently visited any of the following caves in Afghanistan?
a) Tora Bora;
b) Tora Tora Tora;
c) Tory Tory Tory.

10 If you were a car, what make of car would you be?
a) a Chieftain tank; b) an Iranian missile launcher; c) a Volvo Estate (with a bomb in the boot).

11 Is your journey really necessary?

12 Would you like a free copy of the Daily Telegraph?

13 Have you seen Maddy?

14 Have you placed all your toiletries in a clear plastic bag so that the other passengers can laugh at you?

15 Would you like to buy a copy of the Big Issue?

16 Can you read the number plate of an exploding bus at 65 metres?

17 Do you think it'll rain this afternoon?

18 Have you ever been in an aeroplane before? If so, how many times? (State number exactly, giving name of captain in each case.)

19 Is your address still the same as it was when you began filling in this questionnaire?

20 Have you spent so long filling in this questionnaire that you have missed: a) your plane; b) your train; c) your entrance to Paradise to meet the 72 virgins?

That's enough questions. Ed.

"Just a minute, you're not my wife"

CARRY ON BORIS

Is size important, what?

Cheeky!

Cripes! You can't beat a chopper for a bit of fun, eh missus?

Naughty!

Saucy!

No one's going to accuse me of firing blanks!

Are Independent schools pricing themselves out of the market?

by Our Education Correspondent **Conrad Blackboard**

A NEW report expresses the fear that Britain's private schools could be put out of business by soaring, above-inflation fees which now average more than £50,000 a year per pupil.

But last night one of Britain's top headmasters Mr R G J Kipling, of the prestigious Midlands public school St Cakes (motto 'Quis paget entrat'), hit back at critics of the sector's supposedly excessive fee-structure.

"Schools like St Cakes" said Mr Kipling, "have to attract the very best quality teachers, and provide world-class facilities."

"This costs money" the Head said last night from his luxury yacht Academia V, at its mooring in Grand Cayman harbour.

"The parents of our children want nothing but the best, as do I."

"I am proud to say" he concluded, "that St Cakes is now top of the fees league table, with our new termly charges averaging £500,000."

"This means the school now attracts a wide range of Russian oligarchs, Saudi arms dealers and top Chinese Communist party officials."

Full story and league tables pp.16-18.

POETRY CORNER

In Memoriam Norman Mailer, Giant of American Literature

So. Farewell then
Norman Mailer,
Famous for having
Six wives
And many mistresses.

Your most famous book
Was *The Naked
And The Dead*.

Obviously you spent
Much of your life
Being naked.

And now
You are dead.

      E.J. Thribb, (aged 17½)

In Memoriam Karlheinz Stockhausen

So. Farewell
Then Karlheinz
Stockhausen.

Famous modern
Composer.

All together
Now –

*Bing. Bang!
Three-minute silence.
Knock. Knock.
Beep.
Plonk. Bang!
Whirrr...*

I hope I
Have got
This right.

      E.J. Thribb (17½)

In Memoriam Roy Scheider, Hollywood Actor

So. Farewell
Then Roy Scheider,
Star of *Jaws*.

"You're gonna need
A bigger boat."
That was your
Catchphrase.

All together now –
Da-dum *(pause)*
Da-dum *(pause)*
Da-dum-da-dum-da-dum...

      E. 'Jaws' Thribb (17½)

Scenes You Seldom See

"*If we leave now we could get up early tomorrow and go to church*"

"*Would you mind if I put my shirt back on, Dave? I'm freezing...*"

"*I've just bought something I actually like*"

In Memoriam Humphrey Lyttelton, Jazz Trumpeter and Radio Personality

So. Farewell
Then.
Humphrey Lyttleton.
Popularly known
As Humph.

I'm sorry I
Haven't a clue
What to say

Except that
Now you
Have heard the
Last Trump.

      E.J. Thribb (17½,
Mornington Crescent)

In Memoriam Marcel Marceau, Mime Artist

So. Farewell
Then Marcel
Marceau,
Famous French
Mime.

"

"

Yes. That
Was Your
Catchphrase.

      E.J. Thribb (17½)

Lines on the 67th Birthday of TV Cook Delia Smith

So. Happy Birthday
Delia Smith.
You are 67.

I suppose you will
Be going
Down to Tesco
To buy yourself
A cake.

      E.J. Thribb (17½)

CHINESE EXHIBITION OPENS

Age-Old Emperor Seen For First Time

by Our Antiquities Staff **Terry Cotter**

THE 2,000-year-old Lib Dem Ming, known as "The Worst Emperor" today went on show in a conference hall in Brighton.

But members of the public who had been eagerly anticipating the sight of his legendary army of terracotta liberals were disappointed.

Said one, "We expected thousands of these figures, but when we got there, there were only 17 of them."

"We were told they were too fragile to travel, and frankly the hall looked a bit empty."

However the curator of the exhibition explained, "These 17 clay figurines, each dressed in a suit from Marks & Spencer and carrying placards demanding higher taxes on aeroplanes, 4x4s and anyone earning more than they do are an extraordinary glimpse of a vanished world."

HISTORY IN BRIEF

The Emperor Ming, known as "Ming The Useless", took power nearly two millennia ago, with the promise that he would unite the warring factions of his new kingdom to create a unified Greater Lib Dem Empire that would be unstoppable.

He seized power after the downfall of Cha Lee, the popular but drunk emperor who had reigned since he was a boy, but in later life had become dangerously dependent on rice whisky.

To begin with, the old-world Ming, with his courtly ways and reassuring manner, seemed to restore confidence in his millions of subjects. But as time passed, the new emperor became increasingly unsure of himself and took to peering down toilet bowls, as if seeking his salvation in another world.

This led to the hatching of innumerable plots among his terracotta generals, who eventually overthrew Ming and brought his short, unhappy reign to a premature end.

Where You Can See The Worst Emperor

■ **House of Commons**, 12am Tuesdays only **(Admission free)**

■ **National Liberal Club**, all day **(Members only)**

"Life on the estate has become pretty primitive!"

BLONDE WOMAN MARRIES SOMEONE ELSE SHOCK

by Our Entertainment Staff **Dee List** and **Hugh Cares**

THE world of showbiz was stunned last night by the announcement that a blonde woman was going to marry someone else.

Someone Else, 43, is the latest in a long line of people who have married the blonde woman and other husbands include the first one and that other bloke, although she has also enjoyed high-profile relationships with Thingummy, The Boring One With Glasses and Whatshisname-whowasonthatprogramme.

Says the blonde woman, "Someone Else is completely different from all the others. At last I have met Mr Rightwho'snext. This time, I promise, it's for never".

AUTHOR DENIES BLAIR PARALLEL

by Our Literary Staff **Phil Shelves**

BEST-SELLING author Robert Harris today denied that his new novel *Bastard!* was in any way based on the former prime minister Tony Blair.

The plot of Mr Harris's book centres on a former prime minister Toby Chair, who is forced to resign after leading Britain into a disastrous Middle East war, involving the invasion of a fictitious country called Iraq.

The book's villain, Toby, has a thoroughly unpleasant wife, Cheryl Chair, who is a successful human rights lawyer working for a fictitious firm of lawyers called Matrix Chambers in the fictitious City of London.

Insiders who have read the book have been quick to point out the similarities between one of the story's leading characters, the prime minister's gatekeeper Angelica Bunker, described as "svelte, seductive, 45 and previously at school with Toby Chair" and Mr Blair's one-time aide Peter Mandelson *(surely "Anji Hunter"? Ed.)*

Harris In Wonderland

Harris, however, is adamant that there is no connection between any of his characters and members of the previous government.

"I have never heard of Tony Blair," he said, "not to mention his wife. A writer works from his imagination and I began writing my book looking at nothing more than a blank piece of cheque *(surely "paper"? Ed.)*.

What I like about Autumn

by the distinguished commentator **Simon Hefferlump** of the Daily Telegraph

As the leaves on the trees turn to gold and the mists of mellow fruitfulness rise up on every side, our thoughts turn inexorably to the disastrous leadership of the Conservative Party by David Cameron. Poor "Call Me Dave". What a pathetic figure he cuts, with his ridiculous views on melting glaciers and hugging hoodies. And he is made to look even more of a spoiled and stupid sub-intellectual brat by surrounding himself with dolts and morons like the fatuous Osborne and the barking mad Zac Goldsmith. Honestly, why doesn't this dismal lunatic do the decent thing by jumping out of the window and handing over the job of running the Tory Party to someone like Mrs Thatcher?

● Download 'The Hefferlump Vodcast' from telegraph.tv.co.uk or, if you feel you've read this piece too often, switch to another newspaper.

WHERE WAS LADY JANE?
The question all London is asking

by Phil Diaries

A NOTABLE absentee at yesterday's society funeral for top nightclub owner Mark Birlington-Arcade was Lady Jane Templeton-Massingberd the 25-year old step-cousin of Birlington-Arcade's second wife, Lady Arabella Vane-Trumpington-Birlington-Arcade, later the wife of Marmite-to-Referendum Party magnate, Sir James Fishpaste, a friend of the multi-millionaire Greek playboy and Spectator columnist Taki Takalotofcokupthenos, who has entered the long-running feud between members of the Birlington-Arcade family which threatens to lead to a multi-million pound court case over Birlington-Arcade's will, which could possibly force the sale of legendary West End nightery Twytte's in Berkeley Square, whose members over the years have included Frank Sinatra, Princess Margaret, the Aga Khan, Lord Lucan, Shergar *(cont. p. 94)*

"Could we use your toilet, love? They've closed the one in the park..."

THE McCANNS
An Apology

IN RECENT days, in common with all other newspapers, we may have given the impression that the McCanns might in some way have been connected with the disappearance of their daughter Madeleine. Headlines such as *"Police Now Certain That Parents Killed Maddie"*, *"Did They Dump Her In The Sea?"* and *"They Always Looked A Shifty Pair To Us"* may have suggested that we believed that the McCann's were about to be arrested, charged with murder and sent to prison for ever.

We now realise that there was not a jot nor scintilla of truth in these appalling slurs and mendacious smears against two tragically grieving parents who for four months have been trapped in a nightmare of despair. Headlines such as *"Leave Maddy's Parents Alone, For God's Sake"*, *"Clouseau Cops Should Face Gaol, Not Kate and Gerry"* and *"We Always Said That The McCanns Were Innocent"* should leave our readers in no doubt as to our position on this matter.

Tomorrow: Another apology for today's apology.

The Genius That Was Ned Twinky

by Sir Gerald Kaufman

NO ONE had a greater ability to spot talent than Ned Twinky. The first time I submitted a script to his legendary TV programme TW3, he saw at once how brilliant it was and immediately hired me to write all the best things in the show. Who can ever forget my mould-breaking attack on the then Under Secretary at the Ministry of Health, Reginald Weems-Barkworth, or my coruscating satire on the resignation of Sir Maurice Barnstaple from his seat in Bradford and Bingley North sung, of course, by Millicent Martin, who later confided in me that it was the best thing she had ever sung in her whole life. But perhaps Ned's greatest achievement came when he rang me up to tell me how *(cont. p. 94)*

On Other Pages: *The Ned Twinky Who Knew Me* by Everyone Else

(cont. p. 94)

TV Highlights

Michael Palin's 'The New Series'

PALIN sets off on an epic journey, starting on BBC1 and ending up as a free DVD on the cover of the Times. On the way he travels through a variety of weird and wonderful locations, including BBC2, The Discovery Channel, UK Living, UK TV Gold and British Airways Inflight Entertainment (outbound only).

Join Palin for this entertaining voyage round the airwaves where he travels in the footsteps of himself as he goes round some other places.

MODERN NURSERY RHYMES

Postman Pat,
Postman Pat,
Postman Pat and
His wildcat strike.

Early in the morning,
Just as day is dawning,
He turns over and says
I'm not getting out of bed for
this money.

NEXT WEEK: Postman Pat gets the sack.

DAILY EXPRESS
THE WORLD'S GREATEST NEWSPAPER   FRIDAY OCTOBER 12, 2007

MADDY – NEW THEORY
Was She Abducted By Duke of Edinburgh?

By our Conspiracy Staff
Phillipa Front-Page

THE FIRST day of the Diana inquest has produced a startling new theory from top forensic expert Mohamed Al-Fayed. Fayed called for the entire Royal family to be placed in the witness box and forced to account for their movements on the night Maddy disappeared.

A vital new witness, known only as Mr M. Al F. claims he saw Prince Phillips driving a white Fiat Uno over the border into Spain *(cont. p. 94)*

DIARY

CHRIS MOYLES ANSWERS THE BIG QUESTIONS

So Chris, what's it like being famous?

● Normal people, people who aren't celebs but just do normal stuff – normoes, I call them – often come up to me and bother me with shit like, "What's it like being famous?"

That's a big one. What I tell them is the thing about being famous and shit is you're recognised all over the place, even by people who don't actually know you personally and stuff. That's something people who aren't famous don't realise and stuff. Like I can't go into a club wearing my Radio 1 T-shirt with my face on it without people stopping and saying, "Hey, are you that Chris Moyles guy off Radio 1?"

Even when I'm out for a quiet drink with my mates, just sitting quiet talking shite down the local, I only have to start speaking in my normal voice about some of my fellow celebs like Kylie, Sharon, Kate Moss blah blah blah – all big fans of the show and like that stuff – and, you got it, someone from the other side will come over and say, "Are you that Chris Moyles?"

But fame has its pluses. Like you get to rub shoulders – and a whole lot more, if you're lucky, cwoor – with a lot of well fit birds. And that can't be bad, you know and stuff.

Away from the fame and shit are you really just an ordinary decent bloke, Chris?

● Put it this way. Sure, I have mates who are in quotes showbiz close quotes but I also have mates who are just like normal and like sitting in the local catching up on what I'm up to and just talking about me like everybody does. But when you're on TV and radio as much as I am, you're going to be recognised and all that shit, and you've got to deal with it.

You've had some mega celebs on your Radio 1 show, Chris. Talk us through some of the most memorable moments.

● How much time do we have then? There's been a million billion golden moments, like Liam Gallagher coming on the show, and him pulling his trousers down live on air – fucking outrageous, but you've got to hand it to the bloke, I nearly pissed myself laughing. Then we had the lovely Sharon Osbourne on, and I said, cwoor, I'll give you a tenner for Children in Need if you take off your panties, love, and she did that mad laugh of her and said fuck off Moylesy. Classic!

Or the time I had Professor Stephen Hawking on, and we switched off his voice-box for a giggle and did farty noises instead, cracked us up that one did, and took him down a peg or two, or the time Gerri Halliwell came on and I told her to get her tits out, or when I did the whole show sat with a bucket on my head, or when I did a poo into a teacup live on air, or when the Kaiser Chiefs came on and I asked each one of them to name which one of Girls Aloud they'd most like to shag. Before I came along, British radio used to be full of posh wankers with apples up their arses talking about the balance of fucking payments and stuff, but now it's a lot more like real.

So is the licence fee worth it, would you say, Chris?

● You may think I'm shite, that's up to you, but answer me this: I've got eight and a half million listeners think the sun shines out my arsehole, if you'll pardon my Bulgarian. And I have an educational role, by which I mean I learn kids a helluva lot of shite and that. A lot of them's schoolkids, I've had letters from kids of six and stuff saying "love the show, listen to it every morning Chris, and thanks, Chris, 'cos before I started tuning in I frankly didn't have a clue what a bumcrack was or a twat or a shite or a tongue-kiss or a bum wax or a crotchless thong for that matter, and now I know and I've told all me mates at school and now they think I'm cool like you". It's them that makes it all worthwhile.

So now whenever I hear some tit in a poncey suit and fucking tie on Newsnight with a plum up his arse rabbiting on about the licence fee and what a wicked waste and all that shit, I want to shout back, "Fuck off you middle-class wanker. Before my Radio One show, these kids didn't know what to say to one another at break time, they didn't have the language skills, but now they're all saying, "Did you hear fucking Moylesy this morning, how he pissed the shite out of that twat and stuff?" like they were fluent.

And that makes me proud, that makes me very proud indeed. Like, you could say it's a generation what's found their voice, so thanks to the licence fee they've got themselves a proper education and stuff. Communication's the name of the whatever. So how about sticking that up your fat like licence-payer's arse?

As told to C R A I G   B R O W N

'I DID MY BEST'
Knacker's shock claim

by Our Man In Court **Francine Stockwell-Shooting**

INSPECTOR Knacker of the Yard yesterday defended his actions in shooting dead the Brazilian electrician, Jean Charles de Menezes, in a South London underground station.

Questioned by the prosecuting counsel, the Inspector explained, "It could have been a lot worse. After all only one innocent man died. My officers could easily have killed everyone in the carriage, not to mention those waiting on the platform and even the underground staff checking tickets.

"I think we should be applauded," he continued, "for our restraint in very difficult circumstances. After all, the suspect bore an uncanny resemblance to the dangerous terrorist in question.

"Menezes was wearing shoes and trousers and had two eyes and a nose – just like the wanted man."

Inspector Knacker has since been promoted to head of Scotland Yard's crack anti-terrorist unit known as "The Lying Squad."

"I'll just cut the father's cord"

That Honorary Fellowship Citation In Full

SALUTAMUS CAMILLAM PARKUM-BOWLUM NUNC DUCHESSA CORNWELLIAM CELEBRATA ADULTERA PER MULTOS ANNOS CUM CAROLUS PRINCIPIS GALLORUM REX FUTURUS ET FABRICATOR BISCUTUS ORGANICUS ET CETERA ET CETERA QUONDAM FAMOSSISIMA PER CONVERSATIONUM TELEPHONICUM TAMPAXA COMPARISONE SCANDALUM MAGNATUM ET HOSTILITATE IMPLACABILIS DIANA 'PRINCIPESSA CORDIUM' QUIS DICET AD MARTINO BASHIRO 'SUNT TRES PERSONA IN HOC NUPTIALIS' SED NUNC REHABILITUS PER POPULO BRITANNICO RECOGNITA QUA JOLLIA BONA SPORTICA CUM WELLINGTONIS VERMIS ET SKIRTUS TWEEDUS EX OXFAMA ET CIGARETIS CAPSTANIS FORTIS MAXIMUS (NON TIPPUS) SALUTAMUS ET GAUDEAMUS!

"I killed my wife and buried her in the garden today... Does that make me a bad person, Joe?"

Nursery Times

Friday, October 12, 2007

'HEADS MUST ROLL' Says Queen of Hearts

by Our Wonderland Correspondents
Michael White-Rabbit and **Roy Mad Hattersley**
Photos by Alice Liebovitz

THE Queen of Hearts last night gave an official statement on the so-called 'Crowngate Affair'. "Off with his head!" she said, reacting angrily to a suggestion that she was in a bit of a huff about having her picture drawn by Sir John Tenniel. Palace insiders said the Queen was furious at being depicted in a bad mood and *(cont. p. 94)*

Queen seen walking backwards out of portrait sitting

● **Cinderella Enquiry** *New pictures of coach driving away. Was the footman drunk?*

Harry Potter And The Closet Of Secrets

by **J.K. Rowling** *(rewritten by Peter Tatchell to make it more sexually explicit)*

DUMBLEBORE got off the Hogwarts Express early at Clapham Common and moved towards the ill-lit copse in the far corner.

A voice came magically from behind a bush.

"Hello, wizard! Is that a wand in your pocket or are you just pleased to see me?"

Bumblebore dropped his copy of Time Out's pink guide to London and *(cont. p. 94)*

"Sorry, it's mine"

GLENDA SLAGG

FLEET STREET'S STRONGEST DRINK!?!
(surely 'LINK'? Ed.)

■ HATS OFF to the BBC's Queen of Mean, the gorgeous flame-haired questionmistress-in-chief herself!?! Annie Robinson, I'm talking about, Mister!?! And for why is this Dishy Dame in the news? 'Cause she's had the guts to tell her boring has-been of a husband to pack his bags and clear out!?! Millions of us glamorous getting-on-a-bit gals have got a Past-It Penrose in our lives who we'd like to see walk out the door!?! And then we could swap him for a testosterone-fuelled toy-boy half our age!?! Let's all take a leaf out of Annie's Man-Management Manual and shout, "You are the Weakest Husband! Goodbye!"

■ ANNE ROBINSON!?! What a disgrace!?! Just because you've had a facelift and dyed your hair a stupid colour you suddenly think you're God's gift to the opposite sex!?!! You've kicked out poor old Put-Upon Penrose and you think every toyboy in the country will come a-bangin' and a-bonkin' outside your bedroom door!?? Well, I'll let you in on a secret, Annie!?! You still look like the back end of a bus and if anyone is the Weakest Link it's you!?!! If I was Penrose, I'd be down the pub with my mates, having a few beers and chatting up the local talent!??!

ANNE'S DIVORCE SADNESS

I'm having a brave face put on

■ WILLS 'n' Kate – leave them alone, for heaven's sake!?! Ain't it enough that the People's Prince has to relive his Mum's last moments chased by the peeping-tom paparazzi?!? And now he can't even go out with his girlfriend for a quiet curry without being hounded by the hordes of lascivious lensmen a-snappin' and a-pappin'!?!! Next thing we know he'll be crashing into the Kingsway underpass driven by a drunk Frenchman!?!! Is that what we want!?!

■ WILLS 'n' Kate – what do they expect when they go out a-boozin' and a-schmoozin' in the seedy nightclubs of South Kensington?!!?! No wonder the men with the Minoltas come swarmin' around when they hear the heir to the throne is locked in a steamy public embrace with Cutie Kate, his hot date, who just happens to be Mrs Queen-To-Be!!? Clean up yer act, Princey-Boy, and stop yer whingeing. No offence, Sire!?!?

■ HATS OFF to Princess Beatrice!?! At last a glamorous Royal to be proud of, strutting her stuff alongside her gorgeous flame-haired mother who makes Rita Hayworth look like Thora Hird!?!! Good on yer, Princess Beautiful!?!! Geddit?!! You light up our lives Your Ma'amship just like your Auntie Diana!??

■ PRINCESS BEATRICE!?!! What a disgrace!?!! Parading herself up and down the catwalk with her Mum as though she was Kate Moss or her Auntie Diana!?!! It was lucky the catwalk didn't collapse when the two of them came gallumpin' on stage!?!! Take a tip from Auntie Glenda and Bea off with you!?! Geddit?! And as for your Mum, she can Ferg off as well!?! Geddit?!

Byeeee!!!

The 5-second Interview

Marco-Gordon Novelli, television personality & chef

In a nutshell, my philosophy is...

Live for the...

(Sorry, that's all we have time for. Next week: Paris Britney Lohan)

Radio 3

Italian opera

'I detti di Pavarotti'

(sponsored by Northern Rock)

First chance to hear Puccini's long-forgotten opera in which the two wives of a famous opera singer argue over his fortune only to find that he left £12 million of debt. They then fight over who should *not* inherit the debt in the now famous aria, "Your enormous bank account is frozen".

IN THE COURTS

Inquest into the death of the late Diana, Princess of Wales (Day One)

Mr Justice Scott-Carrot: Ladies and gentlemen of the jury. Before we hear any evidence it is my duty to tell you that we are not here to find guilt or to attribute blame.

Mr Fayed: Yes, we fuggin' well are.

Scott-Carrot: Mr Hugefee, will you kindly prevail upon your client to be silent. He will have ample opportunity later to accuse the Duke of Edinburgh of murder.

Mr Hugefee (*for Mr Fugger*): My Lord, my client is an emotional man who after ten long years is still suffering from the effects of lunacy... I am sorry, My Lord, that should have read "grief". I was looking at the wrong bundle. Is it to be wondered at that he occasionally allows his strong feelings to get the better of him?

Scott-Carrot: I am indebted to you, Mr Hugefee, for your lengthy and costly peroration on the origin of Mr Fugger's mental imbalance. Now, if we may continue...

Members of the jury, you may, may you not, have heard the name Princess Diana before – possibly on the televisual device or possibly in the pages of *Hello!* magazine which your wife may have brought home from the dentist, might she not?

But it is my duty to impress upon you that you must eradicate from your memory any image, thought or preconception you may have concerning this unfortunate lady who died in a simple car crash.

Mr Hugefee: My Lord, with the greatest respect, I must object – you cannot prejudge this complex issue which we should be able to spin out for at least six months at the appropriate remunerative rate.

(The other thirty lawyers seated behind Mr Hugefee all begin to cheer and wave their chequebooks)

Lawyers: Hear! Hear!

Scott-Carrot: Gentlemen, I stand corrected. The case is, as you say, far from reaching a clear-cut conclusion or *Res certificatum*.

(Jury look blank).

Members of the jury. I come now to the various conspiracy theories that I have just asked you to banish from your minds. They are the work, you may think, of Mr Fugger, who you may have seen in the pages of the *Daily Express* and you may well have formed the impression that this gentleman is quite obviously off his rocker. If that is what you rightly think, I must again ask you to banish such thoughts from your mind until the time comes, in maybe six months or so, to bring in a verdict of accidental death.

Fayed: Fuggin' Judge! You're working for fuggin' MI6! You're related to Prince Fuggin' Philip!

Mr Hugefee (*sotto voce*): Mr Fugger, I beg you pray silence until His Lordship calls you to the witness box or else he might despatch you to prison where it would be difficult, nay impossible, for you to hand over to me the large brown envelopes full of used notes which form such an important part of our case.

Scott-Carrot: I feel this may be an appropriate time to break for luncheon. Members of the jury, we have had a busy few minutes, have we not, and you may now adjourn. However, I must warn you that once you leave this court you must talk to no one and you will be taken from this place by armed police officers to the nearby McDonalds restaurant, where I am informed you may eat the following items should you so wish: One Big Mac. One portion French Fries. One Shake.

Fayed: I'm not a fuggin' sheikh – I'm the owner of Harrods.

(The case continues)

"Sorry, I think you misread the signs"

THAT LONDON MAYORAL ELECTION MANIFESTO IN FULL

by The Rt Hon Boris Johnson MP, OE

As I cycle around London, or rather I don't because some rotten oik has stolen my bike, I hear some of you chaps (and chapesses, of course) yelling at me, "Oi Boris! We can't take you seriously. You're just a joke!"

Well, hang on a minute! Just because Boris likes to have a laugh doesn't mean he hasn't got a first-rate brain ticking away under his cycle helmet!

Take houses, for example. There's loads of them in London and some of them are jolly expensive. Fair enough. That way you keep out the riff-raff – just the sort of coves who go round stealing a chap's bike when he's left it outside some totty's house when he's popped round for a spot of electioneering! Jolly unfair, what? That's the sort of problem old Boris is going to get *serious* about! You see! So watch out, Ken!

And not just Ken! What about that Lib Dem they are putting up against me? Commander Paddick – Britain's top gay cop.

Now let me make it jolly clear that I've got nothing against gay policemen. But crikey! We can't have a bent copper as Mayor, can we? Blimey! London would be a laughing stock – unlike if it chose Yours Truly!

Abyssinia!!

Here's some more of my Cockney rhyming slang!

Doing the Knowledge – *Eton College*

'ale and 'arty – *Spectator party*

Big Ben – *Goodbye Ken*

Rose & Crown – *Trousers down*

Dog & Duck – *Afternoon tea*

Mr David Cameron
An Apology

IN COMMON with all other newspapers we may have given the impression that Mr David Cameron, the leader of the Opposition, was in some way a born loser, a man of straw and a busted flush who had no genuine convictions and who would be no match for the experienced statesman Mr Gordon Brown in a General Election. Headlines such as "New Gaffe By Useless Cameron", "Another U-Turn By Flip-Flopping Twit" and "Simon Heffer Says Cameron Is Washed Up" may have reinforced readers' perception that we believed Mr Cameron was a less than effective leader of the Conservative Party.

Following his speech at the annual Tory conference at Blackpool, we now realise that Mr Cameron is in fact a towering political figure – a world statesman to rank alongside such illustrious Tories as Sir Winston Churchill, William Gladstone and Demosthenes.

We further accept unreservedly that, had there been a General Election, Mr Cameron would have won by a landslide and would have become the Best Prime Minister since *(You've done this bit. Ed.)*

Mr Gordon Brown
An Apology

IN COMMON with all other newspapers we may have given the impression that Mr Gordon Brown was a towering political figure who, unlike his predecessor, was a man of solid principle whose position as Prime Minister was unassailable and who would easily win any contest he chose to call.

We now realise that there was not a jot or scintilla of truth in any of the above. We are happy to make it clear that Mr Brown is in fact a weak, shifty, dishonest, spin-crazed incompetent who is even worse than Blair. If there had been an election tomorrow he would not have won a single seat.

We apologise for any confusion our earlier reports may have caused.

ON OTHER PAGES: The English Rugby Team – An Apology, Lewis Hamilton – An Apology, etc etc.

"Eating out is always a problem. Chloe's a vegan, little Bobby's wheat intolerant, and Robert only eats ants"

'OBESITY WORSE THAN SMOKING' – GOVERNMENT TO ACT

by Our Nanny State Staff **Lunchtime O'Bese**

HEALTH Secretary Alan Johnson last night announced a new crackdown on the menace of obesity in public places, which he described as "unacceptable in the 21st century".

Said Mr Johnson, "We are going to adopt a policy of zero tolerance towards all people who choose to inflict their fatness upon others."

Fat Lot Of Good

"In future this Government will introduce a total ban on being fat anywhere in public. This includes pubs, restaurants, trains and the workplace.

"If you want to continue with the disgusting habit of being fat, you will have to go outside and huddle together in doorways with other fat people – that is if you can fit in with Dawn from Accounts and Terry from IT – and make sure you don't obstruct anyone or you will be liable to an on-the-spot fixed penalty of £250."

Where You Can Still Be Fat

1. House of Commons
2. Er...
3. That's it

GMTV SHOCK

How much have we been fined?

We're talking telephone numbers

* Loss of 2,000 jobs in TV Production

* Creation of 4,000 senior management posts to facilitate the loss of those 2,000 jobs.

* Er...

* That's it.

"Well, it looks like we've no choice... we'll have to cut the programmes"

From Lord Greed, Chairman of GTV

NO ONE is more distressed than I over the revelations of phone-line fraud concerning Mr Antwell Dec and Mr Declan Ant.

Let me make it clear that whatever is alleged to have happened happened long before I became chairman of Gnome TV. And, even if it didn't, I knew nothing whatsoever about the so-called events at any time.

As is well documented, I have a policy of zero tolerance for people who say I should resign. Or those who suggest that I should reprimand either Mr Decwell Ant or Mr Antlan Dec, whose courtesy titles of Executive Producer in no way implied that they had anything to do with the television entertainment programme bearing their name and starring themselves.

May I reassure everyone that lessons have now been learned and it is unnecessary either to sack any staff or for the police to be involved.

I take full responsibility for none of this. It is all someone else's fault. That, after all, is the motto of the Greed family – "The Big Bucks Stop here."

LORD GREED,
GTV, Cigar House,
Red Brace Road, London

Should we go to jail?

Ring now. Calls charged at £10 per second

IN THE COURTS

'I Saw Flashing Light In Death Tunnel' Claims French Witness

Inquest into the death of the late Diana, Princess of Wales (Day 94). The case was heard by Mr Justice Scott-Carrot, with Mr Michael Hugefee QC acting for Mr Mohamed al Fugger.

Scott-Carrot: Ladies and gentlemen of the jury, I hope you all, like me, enjoyed our agreeable mini-break together in the romantic city of Paris. You may think, may you not, that, with its leafy boulevards, delightful pavement cafes and world-famous Eiffel Tower, there could be no more perfect place to spend the weekend. But, if such be your conclusion, I must ask you to put it from your minds, as it has no bearing on the issues of the case before you.

I must ask you instead to sit back, relax and enjoy this video of our next witness, Monsieur Jean-Jacques Lunie, who cannot unfortunately be present with us to give his evidence in person but has sent us this message from his top-security ward in the Clinique des Imbeciles, Limoges.

M. Lunie *(on video)*: Bonsoir Votre Honneur, et aussi bonsoir à mon vieux ami M. Fugger.

Fugger: Get on with the fuggin' murder and the fuggin' James Bond style laser cannon!!

Scott-Carrot: Mr Hugefee, I must ask you to restrain your client.

Hugefee: My Lord, may I just consult my notes... *(Hugefee counts out notes in wad of used tenners given to him by Mr Fugger)* My client Mr Fugger has no further interjections to offer during the video.

Scott-Carrot: May we now please continue with the video device?

M. Lunie: Imaginez le scene, si vous voulez, quel horreur! Moi dans ma petit voiture, et, voila, c'est la fameuse princesse Anglaise, clairement pregnant par son mari M. Dodi Fugger, dans un Mercedes. Et, soudainment, qu'est-ce que c'est? Une flash de lumiere enorme, comme un bombe atomique. Sacre bleu, j'ai dit à moi-même. C'est le Duc de Edinburgh et ses amis de MI6, ou mon nom n'est pas Jean-Jacques Lunie!

(Mr Fugger here lets out a loud cheer)

Fugger: What did I fuggin' tell you, Your Fuggin' Honour!

M. Lunie *(still talking animatedly on the video while men in white coats attempt to take him away)*: I 'ave not feeneeshed yet. Il faut que je tell you about le monstre de Loch Ness, qui etait aussi dans le tunnel avec son ami M. Darth Vader.

(Here the video went blank)

Scott-Carrot: Well, we have had a very emotional morning, have we not? I must ask you now to say nothing of what you have heard today, even when you read about it in tomorrow's newspaper.

And now might be an ideal moment to adjourn for luncheon, though I have to say that the Garrick Club may not quite rise to the incomparable culinary standards of Le Petit Jardin des Gourmets in the Rue de la Princess Morte, where we all had such an agreeable dinner at the expense of the taxpayer last Tuesday evening.

(The case continues)

'MENEZES WAS COKE-FIEND'
– Knacker's Shock Claim

by Our Crime Staff **Francine Stockwell**

THE BRAZILIAN electrician Jean Charles de Menezes, shot by police at Stockwell underground station, had traces of the banned drug cocaine in his urine, Inspector Knacker of the Yard told a court yesterday.

Said the inspector, "This changes everything. We were right all along. Menezes was no angel, as the media have alleged – he was clearly a junkie, not to say an international drug dealer, who deserved to be executed before he ruined any more innocent people's lives.

"They should be giving my lads a medal for ridding the world of this evil menace, not putting them on trial for some trumped-up health and safety charge just because they happened to kill an innocent man.

"To my mind," said Knacker, "my murder team played their socks off with regard to this one. And I fully deserve my bonus."

"Hi, I'm looking for some 'Northern Soul'. Is it this way?"

"Noooo... not that way. That way Madness lies!!!"

GRAEME KEYES

EXCLUSIVE EYE SERIALISATION

WARTIME HEROES
by the Rt. Hon. Gordon Brown

No. 1

It takes real courage in the middle of a war to stand up and not be counted. Such was the story of a brave Gordon Highlander in the dark days of the Iraqi war who heroically kept quiet, when all around him his colleagues were going over the top. It would have been all too easy to stand in front of his commander and say, "You're wrong – this is madness. If you carry on with this war, I will not support you". But that would have been the coward's way out. That would have been the dishonourable path taken by weak men like Robin Cook. Instead, the brave Gordon Brown remained at his post, keeping his head down and, as a reward, was made Commander-in-Chief. Such valour is rare in our island's story.

Tomorrow: *How Gordon bravely stormed into the Daily Telegraph and fearlessly hijacked Remembrance Day for himself.*

ELDERLY CHINAMAN 'LEFT TO DIE'
Shocking tale of abuse of the old

by Our NHS Staff **M.R.S .A. Bugg**

AGE CONCERN yesterday highlighted the appalling case of an elderly patient who was left to die with no help from those around him.

Mr Ming, 86, had been going downhill rapidly but his feeble appeals for help were callously ignored by his professional carers.

Lib Dementia

Some youthful members of staff even went so far as to poke fun at him in his final hours, joking that he was a 2,000-year-old Chinese emperor who had lost his army.

When Ming was found dead last week, one of his colleagues said "It was entirely Ming's decision. He had always made it clear that he would choose the time when we would turn off his life support system."

Another close colleague said "Ming always wanted to go with dignity. Any suggestion that we had somehow killed him off is as appalling as it is true."

An inquiry is to be held into the circumstances surrounding Mr Ming's tragic demise, since this is the second time in less than two years that a similar fatality has taken place on the notorious Jeremy Thorpe Ward.

A Mr Charles Kennedy was reported to have died of alcohol poisoning, although he was later discovered to have been knifed in the back by an unknown assailant, using an antique Chinese dagger with a handwritten note attached bearing the message "A wee stab afore ye gang".

MING SPEAKS OUT

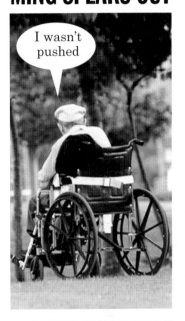

I wasn't pushed

That All-purpose Alcohol Health Scare Story Article In Full

NEW RESEARCH published today has revealed that drinking one glass of red wine a day *is beneficial to your heart and likely to prevent coronaries/ certain to give you any number of cancers.*

It went on to state that pregnant women who drink one glass of wine a day *are not putting at risk the health of their unborn child/certain to give birth to a deformed, brain-dead mutant.*

The report also found that a man drinking more than two glasses of red wine a day would *end up trouserless on a park-bench with the rest of the alcoholics/find it had little impact on his overall health.*

BROWN'S CLUNKING FIST

The Blair Speech That All America is Dying to Hear

(and most of them will)

My fellow Americans,

It gives me great pleasure to be here in this lovely city of (fill in name).

As I was coming here tonight a taxi driver said to me (fill in local joke with punch-line "Aren't you the British guy who appeared on the Simpsons?").

But to be serious for a moment – we are all today facing a new and terrible peril, which reminds me of the dark days of the 1930s when Britain and America stood alone against the weapons of mass-destruction wielded by Adolf bin Laden.

9/11 was the Pearl Harbor of World War Three. It is time for us all to be scared, very scared indeed. Think of a mushroom cloud covering your beautiful city of (fill in same name as city mentioned earlier. IMPORTANT NOTE: if you are in Denver, do not say New Dworkin).

But do not despair, my fellow Americans. All it requires is for Britain and America to stand together as they have done through the centuries, right back to the Battle of Yorktown.

And I give you my solemn promise, as Prime Minister of Britain, that I am ready at any time to join shoulder to shoulder with your great President and my closest friend George W. Bush in the historic task of bombing Iran to smithereens.

Please may I now have my cheque for $250,000?

That Blair US Charity Dinner Menu in full

War on Terrine
Brown Trouser Soup

– ✳ –

Iraq of Lamb with Rehashed Cold Potatoes
Rumsfeld Steak with Warm Onger Sauce
(No Peas in Our Time)
Duck

– ✳ –

Condoleezza Rice Pudding
Trifle Over-The-Top
H-Bomb Surprise

– ✳ –

Selection of Cheese-Eating Surrender Monkeys with
Completely Crackers

– ✳ –

TO DRINK:
Bin Laden Ends from the Cave of Tora-Bora
Nuits St Georges Bush

Ticketholders only: $2,000 per head. Tanks at 12.30 a.m.

THE BOOK OF EHUD

Chapter 94

1. And lo, it came to pass in the land of Gaza, that the Hamasites rose up against the children of Israel.

2. Then they launched rockets into the land of Israel that are called Katyusha, which is to say, "We bought these cheap off Mr Putin".

3. Then Ehud, the leader of the Israelites, waxed wrath and rent his garments and cried aloud saying, "Woe unto ye, ye Hamasites, for ye have verily gone too far this time".

4. And he then sayeth, "Let there be no light".

5. And there was no light. And Ehud saw that it was good.

6. Then darkness fell upon Gaza and the hum of the conditioners of air and the freezers that are called fridges were stilled even as the hum of the desert wasp is stilled when it sleepeth in the desert of Yentob.

7. And Ehud cried again, "Listen to me ye scorpions of darkness and thinketh thou on't".

8. "If thou taketh not heed then next time I will command the waters that they flow not into your land."

9. "And your throats will be parched and your fruit shall whither upon the vine, yea, even your figs shall shrivel and be as food for the swine."

10. "Not that I wouldeth do this obviously, but don't be-eth too sure, thou sons and daughters of darkness."

11. And Ehud rejoiced privily with exceeding great joy and sayeth unto himself,

12. "This is even better than the smiting".

(To be continued forever...)

HOW RETAIL WORKS

He's having his Gap year

"Actually, I only took holy orders to get the kids into a C of E primary"

'We Have No Idea How Many There Are' Admits Immigration Chief

by Our Political Staff **Phil Country**

THE HEAD of Britain's immigration department today confessed that the official figure for the number of idiots in his department was much higher than originally thought.

"There are thousands of them working here," he said, "most of them are completely unskilled and we can't just send them home."

He denied that earlier estimates of the scale of the idiot problem had been deliberately misleading.

"It's very hard to count the true number of idiots here – particularly when you have given the counting job to an idiot."

He concluded, "But don't worry. If you have a problem with immigration remember that my door is always open."

Late news

● THERE was shock today after it was revealed that nearly half of the million and a half new jobs created under this government were being given to British people. "This is intolerable," said a concerned person, "British people should be allowed to sit at home and watch GMTV and Deal or No Deal, and not pick strawberries or work on building sites or serve coffee to *(cont. p. 94.)*

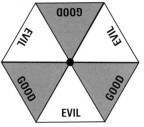

A Cabbie writes

EVERY week a well-known Professor of History is invited to comment on an issue of topical importance. This week: **Prof. Norman Stone** (Ankara Mini-cab no. 3412) on the Kurdish threat to Turkey.

Blimey, guv, those Kurds, they've got a bloody nerve, trying to invade Turkey! After all we've done for them! Know what I'd do with them Kurds. String 'em up, just like we did with them Armenians, not that we did mind you, that's an appalling slur on the good folk of Turkey. Blimey, they'll be stopping us joining the EU next, I had that Kemal Ataturk in the back of the cab once. Very clever man. You didn't bring a bottle of Scotch through Customs did you – I've got a terrible thirst on me.

NEXT WEEK: Sarah 'Slosher' Kennedy (cab no. 621) on the difficulty of spotting black people in the dark until they open their mouths.

2000 Years Ago in the Times

Virgil Resigns Shock

by Our Political Staff
Maximus Hastings and **Sybil Fawlty**

The poet Virgil today handed in his resignation after making remarks which would later be used by the disgraced politician Enoch Powell. In one passage he described the river Tiber "foaming with blood", a deliberately inflammatory reference to the hordes of Nubians, Ethiopians and Carthaginians who are flooding into Rome and taking Roman jobs from Roman slaves.

FULL STORY Aeneid Book 6

LEWIS HAMILTON 'SICK OF HOUNDING'

by Our Formula One Correspondent **Bernie Eccle-not-stunned**

BRITISH F1 motoring sensation Lewis Hamilton has revealed that he is fleeing Britain for Switzerland so that his money can get some much needed privacy.

"My millions can't go into any high street bank without being hounded by fans from the Inland Revenue demanding I pay tax," said a distraught Hamilton.

"I know that my money will never get any peace until I flee the country for a tax haven."

The authorities in Switzerland have promised Hamilton that his millions will enjoy unrivalled privacy far from the prying eyes of Britain's tax men.

HOME OFFICE IMMIGRATION FIASCO

There has been no cover-up

Fnarr! Fnarr!

"I wouldn't – you'll create a culture of dependency"

POETRY CORNER

In Memoriam Joan Hunter Dunn, Muse To The Late Poet Laureate Sir John Betjeman

So. Farewell
Then Joan Hunter
Dunn.

Many people thought
That John Betjeman
Had made up
your name
To rhyme with
"Aldershot
Sun".

But you were
In fact a real
Person.

And now you
Have died.

But you will live on
Forever.

Thanks to the
Immortal lines
Of my fellow
Poet.

E.J. Thribb (17½)

In Memoriam Hugh Montgomery-Massingberd, Obituarist

So. Farewell
Then Hugh Montgomery-
Massingberd.

Obituarist in
The *Daily
Telegraph.*

But alas. You
Are not around
To write
Your own.

E.J. Thribb (17½)

In memoriam Senator Edward Kennedy, iconic US politician

So. Farewell then
Ted Kennedy,
Brother of former President
J.F. Kennedy.

Ok, so you are not dead yet,
But we will
Cross that bridge
When we come to it.

E.J. Chappathribbick (17½)

TOP ROYAL NAMED IN BLACKMAIL SCANDAL

by Our Court Staff **Maddy Tupp**

IN THE most shocking scandal to have rocked the Royal Family for over a century, a very senior member of the Royal Family has been identified at the centre of a sensational blackmail drama involving drugs and sex acts "of an unnatural nature".

Prince Charles

It is understood that the Royal personage concerned may be named in connection with a high-profile coming court case which could shake Britain's monarchy to its foundations.

Duke of Edinburgh

The scandal is said to be so "sensitive" that the Palace has imposed a total blackout on talking to the press, refusing to confirm or deny that the Queen herself was involved in the sordid drugs-and-sex story.

Prince Harry

By last night, however, as London was awash with lurid rumours reaching up to the very highest levels of the Royal Family, an authoritative Australian internet website, www.pommiepooftah.co.au, had already named a man who some years ago worked briefly for a business in which a junior member of the Royal Family owns shares.

The Late Duke of Gloucester

We know the name of this individual but we are unable to reveal it owing to the fact that it is not anything like as interesting as we first thought it might be.

A History of Royal Shame

by Leading Historian
Captain Corelli's Barnett

THIS is not the first time that the good name of the Royal Family has been dragged through the mire of a squalid blackmail case.

In 1897, the young Duke of St Pancras, Queen Victoria's great nephew, was approached by a notorious underworld figure of the time, Captain Harry Silvester, who claimed he had irrefutable proof that the young Royal had been caught cheating at a game of Bezique at the seat of the 14th Marquess of Berkmannanshire.

Captain Silvester demanded "50 golden sovereigns" to secure his silence, adding that he also knew of the young Duke's "close friendship" with the notorious sodomite" Lord Alfred Tennyson, known to his circle as "Lunchtime O'Bosey".

The captain's body was later found washed up on the shore of Wapping Reach, with a note pinned to his cravate reading "I tell you the Duke of Fuggin' Edinburgh did it. Signed 'One who knows', a respected merchant of Port Said".

Worse was to come when in 1932, the then Duke of Windsor was approached by an officer of the Household Cavalry, Captain Larry Silvester, who claimed to have secretly shot 8mm kinematoscope film footage showing the heir to the throne illegally moving his croquet ball in front of the 4th hoop during a spirited and close-fought encounter at Auchtermuchty Castle, the seat of Highland laird, the McKay of McKay.

Silvester also implied that the Duke was "an intimate friend" of Noel Coward the celebrated playwright and cabaret artiste of the day. It was an open secret that Mr Coward – known as "Noelie" to his friends – was (cont. p. 94)

Who Killed Hen Harrier?
"Not I," said Prince Harry,
"With my bow and arry.
I was just having fun,
Shooting peasants with my gun."

Who saw him die?
"I" said the twitcher
"I recognised the bird from its picture,
In my book of the Top 60 British Birds of Prey
Threatened with Extinction."

Who found the bird's body?
"No one" said PC Snoddy
(Of the Norfolk Constabulary)
"Which makes our job very difficult."

Who told the hacks,
By phone or by fax?
"I" said Prince Charles,
"I did the calling,
It really is appalling."

So all the readers of the papers were a-sobbin'
and a-sighin'
As they read the sad story of the Hen Harriers dyin'.

© Prince William McGonagall

I know nothing about these two birds

Ha ha ha, Your Highness

MODEL ECO TOWN

MODEL VILLAGE

That Carter-Ruck Gorbals Bill In Full

P. CARTER-FUCK AND PARTNERS

Commissioners of Oaths and Purveyors of Fine Libel Writs to the Gentry

To: The Taxpayers of Great Britain on Behalf of the Rt. Hon. Michael 'Mick' McGorbals, Speaker of the House of Commons.

To: answering telephone call from Mr McGorbals complaining that the "entire" press was out to get him.
£2,331.11p

To: answering another telephone call from Mr McGorbals asking whether we had seen the Daily Mail today, containing an article by a Mr Quentin Letts headed "Useless Gorbals Hits New Low".
£1,512.62p

To: senior partner's time, logged at 4 minutes, 12 seconds, with Mr McGorbals in respect of the above article.
£2,214.24p

To: telephone call by senior partner to the House of Commons Budgetary Committee to confirm that this bill would be paid in full out of public funds and receiving assurances to that effect.
£1,462.21p

To: stationery, computers, photocopying, chocolate Hob-nobs and other consumables.
£15,864.22p

Shall we say a total of **£23,664.71p**?

An early settlement of this account would be appreciated. Failure to pay within seven days will result in a financial penalty of not less than £35,000 and/or action being taken under the principle of *habeas argentum pro-solicitorensis*.

"Hang on... I don't think it is a mirage"

● Who Are They? – The Top Ten Runners in the Race to Become Leader of Britain's Third Largest Party?

Chris Huhee, 53, high-flying, telegenic Lib Dem shadow spokesman on low-energy lightbulbs and carbon-neutral paperclips. Educated at St Cakes and Oxfam, Huhee is a passionate moderniser whose book *Whither the Euro?* is a seminal Lib Dem text.

Nick Blogg, 40, high-flying, telegenic Lib Dem shadow spokesman on solar-powered wind farms, coastal flood defences and the Single European Fish. Educated at St Cakes and Oxfam, Blogg is a passionate moderniser whose contribution to the famous Tangerine Book entitled *Whither the Euro?* became an iconic text for the Lib Dem awkward squad (Sid and Doris Oaten).

Dick Clugg, 46, low-flying, tele-pathic Lib Dem backbencher and member for the Isles of Silly. Clugg made his name with a passionate speech at the 2003 Lib Dem Conference calling for a tax on trouser presses imported from China as a contribution to the fight against global warming.

Alison Yoghourt, 46, even-lower-flying, telescopic former Lib Dem MEP from Humberside. Educated at St Crumpet's School for Girls and the Rolf Harris School of Art, Nuneaton, Yoghourt made her name piloting the Moth Quota scheme through the Strasbourg parliament.

● *That's enough Lib Dem high-flyers, Ed.*

"Come on... come on... come ON!"

Godot.com.

Nursery Times

.... Friday, November 9, 2007 ....

PUNCH AND JUDY TO LOSE DAYTIME SHOW

by Our Media Staff **Emily Ding-Dong-Bell**

THE long-running Punch and Judy show is to be axed from the schedules, it was revealed last night.

Afternoon viewers have been entertained for years by the antics of Richard Punch and his wife Judy, who bicker with each other whilst interviewing celebrity guests such as policemen, crocodiles and dogs carrying strings of sausages.

Said a spokesman, "The format has become tired and repetitive, so we are hitting it on the head." He concluded, "That's the way to do it, boys and girls."

● **On other pages**:
"Eating flies bad for you"
– Doctor tells old woman
"Thumbs give you cancer"
– Little Jack Horner warned
"Four and twenty blackbirds"
– Nigella's exciting new recipe
● **Have you seen Hansel and Gretel?**

Court Circular

(Sponsored by Bae Systems)

Buckingham Palace, Tuesday

His Supreme Highness and Custodian of the Fourteen Million Holy Oil Wells, King Abdullah-Abdul-bin-al-Fayed of Saudi Arabia, today commenced a State visit in London to Her Majesty the Queen and HRH the Duke of Edinburgh.

A procession was formed as follows from Heathrow Airport to the Palace.

1st Coach
(The Edward VII Imperial Coronation Landau)

HM The Queen and His Majesty King Abdullah

2nd Coach

HRH Prince Philip, accompanied by their Royal Highnesses the Princes Abdul-al-Shufti, Mohammed-al-Shifti and Asif-al-Shafti

1st Armoured Car

Chief Bodyguard to the Custodian of the Holy Oil Wells, General Prince Rashid-al-Bashem-al-Smashem and Chief Inspector Knacker, Commander of the Queen's Own Protection Squad

1st Rolls Royce

Sir Alan Fitztightly, Equerry to the Old Queen, accompanied by the Blackmailer Royal Mr Ian Sleazeball, Prince Wasim-bin-Laden-al-Qaeda, Head of His Majesty's Very Special Forces Overseas and Lady Laetitia Starborgling, Mistress of the Queen's Hatpins

First Open-Top Bendy Bus

His Holiness the Imam Khalifa of Jihad, Head of Wahabi Export Studies at the University of Mecca, and the Rev. J.C. Flannel, Chair of the Interfaith Liaison Committee of the Church of England

First Camel

His Highness Prince Q'ruki, Keeper of the Royal Backhanders

Second Camel

Mr Roger Browne-Envelope, Contract Facilitation Department, Bae Systems, Riyadh

First Man with Placard

Mr Hugh Man-Rights (subsequently arrested by Inspector Knacker and held for 28 days under the Prevention of Terrorism Act 2005)

First Bicycle

Mr Boris Johnson, prospective candidate for London Mayor, having lost his way to the House of Commons after spending an agreeable afternoon discussing London transport issues with Miss Samantha ('Sam') Starborgling, daughter of Lady Laetitia *(see above)*

There was then a ceremonial fly-past of RAF Eurofighters, towing a banner bearing the legend 'Buy One, Get One Free'. This was followed by a fly-past of rare Hen Harriers which were shot down by HRH the Prince Harry, accompanied by his friend Count Heinrich von Ricketson-Smythe O.E.

That Buckingham Palace Menu in full

Crude-oil-ités
Brown Nose Windsor Soup

– ✳ –

Halal Fish Fingers (in Till)
Appease Pudding
Choice Cuts of Hand (off the bone)

– ✳ –

Roast Sucking-up Pig
Tornados of BAeef with Gravy Train
Torture Rack of Lamb on a Behead of Lettuce

– ✳ –

Arabian Dessert
Bread and Buttering-Up Pudding

– ✳ –

TO DRINK:
Al Quaeda-free Beer
Assorted Milked Sheikhs

The band of the Welsh Guards then played the following programme:

Strictly Cwm Rhondda

A Star Wars-on-Terror medley, including The Imperial Stormtroopers March and the theme tune from Return of the Jeddah

♪ and ♫

A selection from the musical Seven Bribes For Seven Brothers

The Secret DIARY OF SIR JOHN MAJOR KG aged 64 ¾

Sunday a.m.

I am not inconsiderably pleased to be invited on the Andrew Marr TV show which is like the David Frost Show except with Andrew Marr rather than David Frost. But, as I pointed out to my wife Norman, unlike David Frost, Andrew Marr does not have a breakfast cereal named after him. "Oh no," she replied, "but he does have a chocolate bar named after him. Oh yes." This was to my mind a foolish remark, neither funny or helpful.

On the show Mr Marrs asked me if in my judgement Mr Blair had been right to accuse my government of sleaze. I was in no small measure incandescent with rage and I said to Mr Marrs, "How dare Mr Blair accuse me of sleaze when his government have a sleaze record second only to my own?"

Mr Marrs was not inconsiderably silenced by my admonition. His only response was to laugh, hold his sides and ask me if I fancied a curry. This was a very silly remark since we had only just eaten our very pleasant breakfast of Golden Grahams (not Frosties) in the BBC Canteen.

21

MARGATE HORROR

HOW MANY MORE BODIES WILL THEY FIND?

● WE don't know.

PLUS MURDER, SEX, GORE, DEATH, SPECULATION 3,4,5,6,7,8,9

PLUS Real news 94

Daily Mail

FRIDAY, NOVEMBER 23, 2007

NEW MURDER THREAT TO HOUSE PRICES?

By Our Property Staff
Bill Board

PROPERTY prices could tumble according to estate agents if more murder victims are uncovered in back gardens.

A leading property expert said yesterday, "Murder could have serious repercussions on the value of your house. If prospective buyers are worried that there might be murder issues with their desired property they should check with the police before completion of the purchase."

"Otherwise the whole property market could go into meltdown."

Mail Case Study

Typical suburban semi-detached two bedroom house

Without body	**£395,000**
With body	**2p**

"I live at the top of the street – can your son turn down his iPod?"

"I don't believe it, man – my mum has taped EastEnders over my martyrdom video"

POLLY FILLER
salutes Nigella

DOESN'T Nigella look marvellous? Like all other women in Britain I've been thrilled to see that gorgeous sexy Nigella is back with even more curves than ever! She is an inspiration to us all, big, buxom and beautiful and brave enough not to care about a few extra pounds here and there (well mostly there!!).

SHE'S sending out a clear message to all us working mums trying to juggle kids, career and cooking – eat all the pies you want – and the cakes too – and drown them in cream and chocolate and lard for good measure! And it really doesn't matter if you start filling out a little and going up a dress size or three! Because Nigella doesn't care how big her bum looks on TV! She's not counting calories or worrying that she is going to break the bathroom scales.

THAT'S why sad middle-aged men like the useless Simon still turn over from James May's Extreme Pipe Smoking on UK Dave 24 Gold to try and catch a glimpse of her dumplings on Nigella Excess on BBC2! But we women love her too. Because she's feisty, fulsome, fleshy and let's face it... FAT! Yes, that's the secret of her success – she makes the rest of us feel thin! Thanks Nigella, for the women of this country you're a genuine Roly-Poly Model!

© Polly Filler 2007.

Sixty Things You Didn't Know About The Royal Couple

The Royal couple received 7,000 wedding presents, including two elephants, a zebra, a U-Boat (from Prince Philip's brother-in-law Count Klaus von Nuremberg) and a trouser press from the people of Corby.

The Royal couple are avid television viewers and their favourite programmes have included: *Crossroads, Bonanza, Jim'll Fix It, Top Gear* and *Imagine* with Alan Yentob.

Prince Philip and the Queen have matching bathrobes, one inscribed "'is" and the other "'ERs".

The Queen loves doing impersonations and does a very good one of Helen Mirren.

Prince Philip hates corgis and once shot twenty in one morning.

The Queen is allergic to swans and refuses to eat them, even at Royal Feasts in her honour.

Prince Philip's pet names for his sons are "Useless", "Thicko" and "Nancy Boy".

The Royal couple have climbed all the world's greatest mountains together – except Everest, which they plan to do next year.

The Queen and Prince Philip are world-class Scrabble players. The Queen once scored 3,987 points with a triple word score for "xylophone".

Although the Duke comes from Greek, Danish, German and English stock, he speaks none of these languages.

On a visit to the Gilbert and Sullivan Islands in 1958 the Duke of Edinburgh was kidnapped by a

HOW THEY STAYED MARRIED

Have you come far?

And what do you do?

troupe of bare-breasted dancers who believed that he was a fertility god. He was only released after the Queen paid a ransom of 28 watermelons and a bowl of fish.

However, there are those who say that the man who was returned was in fact an actor working for the Russians and that the Duke of Edinburgh is now the Head of Smersh (*That's enough made-up facts. Ed.*)

A Message From Your Next London Mayor
BORIS CALLING!!

Make no mistake. It's Boris to the rescue! With my new slogan – *"An end to gum crime in London"*! Not bad, eh? *"Stick with Boris – and not to the pavement!"* Even better!

Boris

What's on Boris's agenda this week? It's the Big One. Chewing gum. Urgh! Frightful stuff, what? Sort of thing oiks spit out on the pavement every day, leaving a nasty, gungy patch of goo for yours truly to step in. Cripes! And what does Red Ken do? Nothing. He's too busy killing the pigeons, sucking up to some Commie dictator like Chavez and sticking up for PC Plod when he goes round murdering innocent Brazilians.

Here's some more of my Cockney rhyming slang!

Dog and Boner – *Matthew D'Ancona*

Jekyll and Hyde – *Bit on the side*

Jolly Good Feller – *Petronella*

Dog & Duck – *Morning coffee*

DEMOCRACY RUSSIAN STYLE

You put a cross... over your opponent's head!

Those Russian Elections In Full

Vladivodka North: Leonid Smersh (Putin For Czar Alliance) 738,462; Boris Bumpdoff [Deceased] (Democratic Freedom Party) 3. *(No change)*

Abramovich South: Sergei Oligarchski (Suicide Party) 2; Polonoim Arslikov (United Putin For Ever Or Else Party) 3,748,798. *(Swing to Putin)*

Putingrad (formerly St Petersburg): Alexander Lunatikov (Gulag Party) -10°C; Vladimir Putin 600,000,000 *(Putin Gain)*

(That's enough results. Ed.)

"Better put these on the top shelf..."

YR

"I didn't mean for you to push that hard"

YES! IT'S OFFICIAL! St Pancras Train Time Smashed!

by Our Man on Platform 9, **Hugh Rowe-Starr**

THEY SAID it couldn't be done, but today I saw with my own eyes the miracle of engineering technology that has made the world suddenly a smaller place. I was there at St Pancras and yet, just 2½ hours earlier, I had been at Waterloo Station.

It didn't seem possible, but as the underground train ate up the miles in what was to be a record-breaking run, passengers whooped and cheered as they opened bottles of champagne to celebrate their arrival.

"I never thought we would ever get off that bloody train," said one.

"You should try the bus," said another. "It's even bloody worse."

Make no mistake. Britain can be proud today as it races ahead into the 19th Century and *(cont. p. 94)*

Lines On The Unveiling Of A Statue of the Late Sir John Betjeman at the Opening of the Newly-Restored St Pancras Station

⟶ by Himself ⟵

What's going on on Platform Nine?
That used to be the Ebbsfleet Line.
But now they've done it up in style
It beats the old place by a mile.

And there's a brand-new Champagne Bar
For those who go by Eurostar.
To Paris and back in half a day,
It's enough to take your breath away!

But what do I see on Platform Three,
A statue that they've made of me!
And all because I saved the station
From catastrophic devastation.

So there I'll stand for years to come,
And kids will say, "Who's that there, Mum?
That funny man in the silly hat,
I wonder what he thinks he's at?"

"Now, come on Kylie, come on Wayne,
Get moving or we'll miss the train."

(Not very good, is it? Put put it in if you like. J.B.)

ME AND MY SPOONY-WOON

RUSSELL BRAND

Do you have a favourite spoon?

I've 'ad thousands of spoons, haven't I? I've 'ad them all... short spoons, tall ones, skinny ones. I've been a right old spoonbender in my time guvnor, if you get my drift, and done things with spoons that I never oughtn't not to have done neither if it so pleases you.

So how did you conquer your spoon addiction?

I went to Spoony jail didn't I where they stop you dunkin' your spoony-woon for a month, so help me if they didn't, in the hope of curing my obsessive spoonophilia if you get my drifty-wift, as dear old Anthony Burgess might say.

Has anything amusing ever happened to you in connection with a spoon?

No-y-wo.

NEXT WEEK: *Russell Crowe. Me and My Crowe.*

24

THE GREAT DONATIONS SCANDAL
The Eye's at-a-glance guide to who gave what to whom
by Phil Coffers

married to

Baroness Jay, supported Hilary Benn in Deputy Leadership contest

£1 million

rejected by

Hilary Bean (TV's Mr Benn), comic Labour minister, son of Bill and Benn, famous Labour flowerpots

Peter Mandelson, long term enemy of Gordon Brown

never heard of

Hillary Clinton, close friend of Tony Blair and frequent visitor to Downing Street

supported

associated with

David Abrahams, at the heart of Labour's web of intrigue

never met

Janet Kidd, Tory-voting secretary of David Abrahams

Felix Mendelssohn, 19th century composer famous for wedding march

Peter Who, teenage General Secretary of the Labour Party, forced to resign

£500,000

related to

£50,000

never met

Harriet Harman, Deputy Leader of the Labour Party, who Abrahams claimed was married to him in 1983

£350,000

Jon Mendelsohn, chief Labour fundraiser and former lobbyist

Jack Dromey, Labour Treasurer, claimed to be married to Blair fundraiser Baroness Jay

associate of

Bob the Builder, influential North Eastern Labour councillor

Labour

(That's enough Web of Intrigue, Ed.)

Harold Abrahams, runner who accepted gold medal in 1924 Olympics

---

KNACKER TO INVESTIGATE 'DODGY DONORS'
by Our Crime Staff **Gordon Brown-Envelope**

CHIEF INSPECTOR Knacker was last night called in again to investigate claims that the government have been acting illegally.

Said Inspector Knacker, "We are confident that we can make a speedy investigation into this matter which will last only two years. After that it will be up to the Criminal Prosecution Service to decide that no further action should be taken and that everyone involved is innocent."

He then promised, "Rest assured I shall do everything in my power to keep my job."

LATE NEWS
● Brazilian electrician shot on suspicion of "donating money to Labour Party" p94.

"How generous – a donation"

OXFORD UNION

Forthcoming Debates

"This House believes in the freedom of the President of the Union to get a lot of publicity by inviting ridiculous and unpleasant people as speakers"

SPEAKERS

For The Motion
President of the Union: Luke Twytte
Treasurer of the Union: Lucy Twytte *(no relation)*

Also for the Motion
Mr Osama bin Laden
President Robert Mugabe
The Late Adolf Hitler

Against The Motion
Everyone else

Members are invited to bring their own placards and to indulge in any form of behaviour which will result in photo opportunities for the President, Mr Luke Twytte

---

THE DAILY TELEGRAPH

Letters *to the Editor*

SIR – Whilst I abhor the opinions of Mr Irving Berlin and Mr Sid Griffin, it is nonetheless their perfect right to express their repulsive views in whichever forum they choose. Surely the way to oppose these loathsome individuals is to engage them in rational debate over a glass of sherry in the attempt to persuade them to adopt a more moderate position.
Dr J. Pangloss,
St Ivel College, Cambridge.

SIR – I am a profound believer in the freedom of speech and those who attempted to silence Sir Oswald Mosley and his friend Herr Mussolini at the Oxford Union last week were guilty of gross discourtesy to two very fine Christian gentlemen. Indeed, in a more enlightened age those protestors would all themselves have been silenced by a healthy dose of capital punishment.
Rear-Admiral Sir Barrington Frisbee,
Berchtesgaden-on-Thames.

SIR – Talk about the right to free speech. What about the extreme right to free speech?
Mike Giggler,
Via email.

A Taxi Driver writes

Every week a well-known taxi driver is invited to address the Oxford Union on a subject of topical importance. This week **David 'Dave' Irving** (minicab no. 19391945) on the holocaust.

Blimey guv, it's obvious innit? Them Jews made it all up. I've been through all them lists and documents and pictures and stuff – hey, they're all fake. And anyway, if they'd killed all them Jews, there wouldn't be any Jews left, would there? How do you work that one out?

I had that Albert Speers in the back of the cab once. He told me that it never happened and he had nothing to do with it. So who are you going to believe, me and my mate Albert, or all those students with beards and stuff?

You know what I'd do with all them troublemakers? I'd gas them, just like they did to the Jews.

That Blair Chinese Speech in full

Good people of (fill in name of city or administrative region).

As I was coming here tonight a taxi driver said to me, "Are you that Tony Blair? You all look the same to me." (Pause for laughter).

No, but seriously, we are all the same in the new global economy. The progress you have made in your country – and particularly in (repeat name of city or administrative region) – is an inspiration to us all.

As prime minister of Britain, I am keenly aware of how much we owe you! $200 billion at the last count! (Pause for laughter).

No, but seriously, we are looking forward to the Olympic Games... showcase for your entrepreneurial achievements... Murdoch satellite TV... jolly good thing... hi-tech... modern architecture... envy of the world... (note to self, don't mention Tiananmen Square, Tibet, human rights, global warming etc.).

So, in conclusion, may I say that this wonderful new development (fill in name of shopping mall, executive flat complex, business park, nuclear power station, landfill site, student prison etc.) is the greatest Chinese achievement of all. (Wait for applause and cheque for £250,000).

And can I end by quoting the words of my host who remarked that a speech by **me** is like a Chinese meal. Once you have had one you immediately don't want another one. (Is this right? Please check. T.B.)

UK'S BASRA TRIUMPH

We're handing over lack-of-control

BASRA 2003   BASRA 2008

HUNTEY

MAJESTY

(as seen on the BBC)

(Pic of Royal Standard rising over Buckingham Palace. Elgar-style music swells in background)

Voice Over: Never before has Her Majesty allowed such intimate access to a film crew. But now the Royal Family, like many other institutions, must adjust its traditional reticence to the demands of the 21st century media.

(Shot of table being laid for 194 people. Close-up of man wiping knife with napkin. Caption: 'Edward Claridge – Senior Knife-Cleaner at Buckingham Palace since 1949)

Claridge: 194 people is about average for when Her Majesty entertains. Tonight we've got the President of Burundi, who is an African gentleman.

(Cut to man in kitchen shelling prawn. Caption: 'Clarence Edwards – Keeper of the Prawn Cocktail since 1921')

Edwards: 194 may sound like a lot of prawn cocktails, but when you've been in the service of Her Majesty for as long as I have you get used to it.

(Shot of guests arriving at reception before dinner)

Voice Over: It's the big moment...

(Close-up of the Queen with crown and full regalia walking into room – not OUT of room: note BBC controller)

Queen: Have you come far?

President of Burundi: From Burundi, Ma'am.

Queen: And what do you do?

President of Burundi: I'm the President.

Queen: How very interesting.

(Cut to President of Burundi five minutes later)

Voice Over: What was it like meeting the Queen?

President: She's a wonderful person. Very natural and really interested in what you have to say. She put me at my ease immediately by asking me whether I had come far and then she enquired what I did for a living.

(Cut to shot of large armour-plated car drawing up outside Buckingham Palace)

Voice Over: But it's not all prawn cocktails for Her Majesty. Every week the Queen receives in audience the Prime Minister of the day. She has known 27 in her reign, going back to the Duke of Wellington.

(Shot of man in suit looking shifty)

Tony Blair *(for it is he):* May I ask you if you are looking forward to your State visit to America, Ma'am?

Queen: And what do you do?

Blair: Ha ha ha ha, Ma'am. I understand it's quite a while since you were last there?

Queen: Oh yes. I met the President, Abraham Lincoln, who was absolutely charming.

Blair: How very interesting, Ma'am.

(There is an awkward pause)

Queen: Have you come far?

(Cut to New Dworkin, State Capital of Virginia. We see an elderly man hoovering a lawn outside the 18th century courthouse. Caption: 'Horace Clambake, Chief Lawn Supervisor, Public Works Department, State of Virginia')

Clambake: The Queen of England coming to New Dworkin. That's something special for us folks. It's history in the making.

Voice Over: They are even installing a new toilet at the New Dworkin Holiday Inn, where Her Majesty is staying.

(Cut to man wearing baseball hat and overalls putting up marble towel rail in toilet. Caption: 'Zebedee Greenberg, Manager, Holiday Inn, New Dworkin')

Zebedee Greenberg: The Queen of England coming to New Dworkin. That's something special for us folks. It's history in the making.

Voice Over: But the big worry turned out not to be the toilet, but the weather.

(Music plays 'Singing In The Rain'. Shot of grey clouds over courthouse)

Voice Over: Would it rain on New Dworkin's big day? Next week we find out...

(More Elgar-style music plays over credits)

© Really Dull Films for the BBC 2007

Daily Mail

FRIDAY, DECEMBER 7, 2007

BIG HEADLINES CAUSE HOUSING SLUMP SHOCK

By Our Economics Staff
Charles Mooregage

SENIOR analysts at the Daily Mail today warned that enormous headlines may lead to a collapse in house prices leaving first-time buyers stranded at the bottom rung of the property ladder.

Said one typical couple, Mr and Mrs Made-up-in-the-office,

"We are at our wits end. If headlines keep getting bigger we'll have nowhere to live at Christmas."

Full story and pictures **p3**

MAN ARRESTED FOR 'LOOKING AT LANGHAM PICTURES'

by Our Crime Staff **P.D. O'Phile**

A MAN who cannot be named for legal reasons has admitted looking at images of Chris Langham, although he claims he only did it "for research purposes".

The man saw the images in the Observer newspaper as well as on BBC TV, under the title *'My Child Porn Hell By TV Star'*.

"I feel ashamed now," said the man. "I looked at the pictures, but surely no one could imagine that I got any pleasure out of it.

"The only possible reason for looking at these awful pictures of Chris Langham is to try and imagine why anyone would give him the opportunity to claim that he was innocent all along *(cont. p. 94)*

"Flippin' kids..."

27

"I've got an eye for the ladies"

"Hello, sailor!"

Now only one farthing!

Daily Victorygraph
— Dec. 1805 —

Visit Trafalgar Square when it's built – fun for all the family

LOVE RAT ADMIRAL IN LEGOVER STORM

By Our Naval Staff Kathy Lette-Me-In

Admiral Horatio Nelson, the one-eyed national security chief, has been revealed as a serial Lothario who has betrayed his long-suffering wife Lady Nelson with a series of secret trysts with glamorous brunette temptress Emma Hamilton.

Kiss me anyone!

The Victorygraph accepts of course that no impropriety took place between the distinguished hero and his good friend Lady Hamilton.

But last night sources close to Lady Nelson said: "Lord Nelson is a bastard. He could not keep his hand off that scheming trollop."

The Victorygraph says it is a scandal that this man is allowed to

exercise responsibility over Britain's defences at a time when we are engaged in a "war against terroir".

Full non-story   p94.
Unfunny cartoon by Gilray   p95.
Your Train Tonight: Mr Stephenson's Rocket will be arriving in 25 years' time.

"I didn't know what to do... he's still waiting to get through to a call centre"

Great British Heroes

—— No. 94 ——

Gordon Brown of Khartoum

HE STOOD courageously at the top of the steps. Below him the angry mob demanded the head of teddy bear teacher, Mrs Daphne Frobisher. Defiantly Gordon stared into the maddened eyes of the crazed Sudanese rabble.

"Look," he said firmly, gathering all his British sang-froid, "I appreciate that we have our cultural differences and I hope that we can solve this amicably through the normal channels."

If you would like to buy a copy of this print, send £250,000 anonymously to the Labour Party at once.

BEAR STORM GROWS

by Our Religious Correspondent **Rupert Bear-Murdoch**

MILLIONS of angry commuters took to the streets of London yesterday in protest at the naming of a teddy bear after their revered railway terminus.

"How dare they call a bear Paddington," protested one extremist railway traveller, "it is sacrilege."

Fur Trials Abroad

Chanting First Great Western passengers beseiged bookshops throughout Britain, waving placards calling for children's book author Michael Bond to be given forty lashes or preferably to be hung from a crane.

Appearing on *Newsnight*, the Peruvian ambassador said, "there is no way I can intervene to save Mr Bond from his deserved punishment. You have to understand that the British have a very different culture from us, and hold their railway system in very high regard."

STOP PRESS

There was more outrage from religious groups yesterday as Hindus protested against the controversial naming of 'Yogi' bear.

"It's obvious that someone at Hanna Barbera has made a huge Boo-Boo," said one beardy *(cont. p94.)*

GNOME PRODUCT RECALL

'The Fugger Bear'

(No. 7342842B)

The cuddly *Fugger Bear* has been recalled following a number of complaints. We now realise that it was inappropriate for the bear to be called 'Mohamed Fayed' and offensive in the extreme for it to shout "The Duke of Edinburgh fuggin' did it!" when pressed on his tummy.

We apologise to our customers and promise to destroy all the remaining *Fugger Bears* in the Gnome Warehouse.

DIARY

ALAN YENTOB

● Catch up on the latest Coen Brothers movie. They're brothers – as the name implies – and interesting with it. One of the great things about all the best movies is that they tell a story, a narrative. And they ask the viewer to become involved in that narrative. That for me is the key to all the finest movie-making – and it's something my friends Joel and Ethan know instinctively.

● Catch up on the latest work of Damien (Hirst). It's truly mind-blowing, something that makes us think again about what we think we already know. Over drinks at the Met, I ask Damien what's he's planning to do next, and he tells me. It's a brilliant idea, and one that I hope will very soon come to fruition. Art is all about ideas – and Damien, like Leonardo (diCaprio) is today considered one of its foremost practitioners.

● Catch up on the latest of yesterday's TV before breakfast. Nigella, *EastEnders*, Graham Norton, Clarkson – let no-one tell you there's not talent out there. To me, it's like living in downtown Florence during the Renaissance – that great period in history when arts controllers and editors were given their own remit and allowed to flourish.

It makes me think we should stop categorising TV into so called 'good' and 'bad'. There are lots of different forms of TV and to me it's all good, even if some of the good programmes are in some way 'bad' in some people's eyes. What defines a TV programme? Well, it is generally – but not exclusively – a programme which has been – or will be, or is being – seen on television. And that's it's special magic, which we underestimate at our peril.

● Catch up on the latest Philip Roth while in the taxi to a meeting with Gilbert and George, to catch up on their latest mammoth artwork, the truly magnificent SodArse, made entirely out of used faeces and tulips. While catching up on the Roth – and, take it from me, it's truly irresistible, what a great writer he is, enjoying a brilliant Indian summer – I catch up on the latest Arctic Monkeys on my iPod, and am once again amazed by those guys' versatility and sheer youthful energy. Catching up on the Arctics, I manage to catch up on my latest Armani suit at the same time: a fine new ultra-contemporary cut, retro-modernism at its best.

● To New York, New York – otherwise known as the Big Apple – to catch up on the latest exhibitions in the famous Chelsea district and to chair a few more cutting-edge committees. It's true to say that BritArt is taking the BA (Big Apple) by storm, and Keith Tyson's brilliant, epic installation at the Pace Wildenstein Gallery is as brilliant and epic as ever.

Hook up with Charles (Saatchi) and Mick (Jagger) in a gaff to eat a brilliant, epic soft-shell crab and to chew over a number of relevant issues concerning the arts, global warming and Britney with Bobby (de Niro) and Al (Gore), among others. Suddenly, everything seems possible in New (York). That's the magic of the place. I once heard someone say it's so great they named it twice.

● Back in *Londra*, I catch up with the 100th edition of *Granta*, which lets me catch up with the latest brilliant, epic love poem by Harold (Pinter) to Antonia (Fraser):

I shall miss you so much when I'm dead,
The loveliest of smiles,
The softness of your body in our bed.
And if ever anyone should pretend otherwise
You should just tell them to fuck the fuck off
Or you'll come round and splash their brains
Over the fucking pavement, just like Bush.

Once again, a work of undoubted genius.

● Catch up with the latest from Salman – the guy's a magician with words, a master storyteller at the peak of his powers, the Amy Winehouse of the printed word.

● And so home, where I catch up on the latest dishwasher by Zanussi, not to mention a brilliant, epic new scrubbing brush by top designer Peter Jones and a truly monumental bar of soap by Camay. For me, Camay continues to reinvent itself, brilliantly blurring the line between art, design, high finance and personal hygiene. Isn't it time we as a society stopped worrying about what is art and what isn't?

As told to CRAIG BROWN

Turner Prize Given To Bore Man

by Our Arts Correspondent
Richard Dormouse

THE world's most coveted art prize was last night awarded to Mark Wally, for a two hour video showing him dressed up as a bore.

Wally, 36, put on a bore suit and was interviewed by hundreds of journalists, talking about himself. "When I act out the role of a bore," he said, "I am making a statement about what it is to be a bore."

What do you think of the Bore Man? Is it art or is it just boring? Are you pro- or anti- bore?

Comment now on our online Boreblog at www.filluptomorrowsindependent.co.uk

What You Won't Be Taking The Children To This Christmas

THAT STEPHEN FRY PANTO IN FULL

★ C I N D E R F E L L A ★

(Enter Buttocks)

Buttocks: Hello boys and boys!

Sandi Toksvig *(with moustache)*: Hello girls and girls!

Audience: It's behind you!

Buttocks: That's the way I like it!

(Enter Prince Charming carrying a slipper. Enter Ugly Sisters)

First Ugly Sister: Let's see if we can *slip* this one in!

Second Ugly Sister: Ooh! Is size important?

Prince Charming: It is to me, ducky!

(Enter Kevin Spacey, artistic director of the Old Dic Theatre)

Spacey: It's all about bums and seats!

Prince: Cheeky!

Audience: Isn't this a bit crude?

Spacey: Oh no it isn't!

Audience: Oh yes it is!

Prince: Ooh! Er! My pumpkin is swelling up! Time for a sing-song!

(Entire cast sing well-loved traditional panto song "FRY-MCA" by the Hampstead Village People)

All *(with actions)*: FRY-MCA! etc.

(Interval during which half the audience rush for toilet, the rest for the exit)

Do you think this panto reinforces gay stereotypes? Or do you think it is ironically affirmative of alternative lifestyles? Send your views to www.pinkpanto.org

CHRISTMAS PICK

FILMS

St Cakes The Movie (2007)

RAUNCHY remake of the original 1954 Ealing classic. This time the boys of St Cakes run riot setting up a crackhouse in the boys' dormitory. Russell Brand takes the Alastair Sim role as headmaster Mr Kipling and Jordan takes the Joyce Grenfell role of Mrs Titzowt, the East European hockey mistress turned lap dancer.

Watch out for the girls from St Crumpets, the sister independent fee-paying school, in suspenders and stockings who plan to get some publicity for themselves and *(That's enough film, Ed.)*

They Flew To Bruges (2007)

ANIMATED remake by Pixel of the 1947 black and white classic. In this version the RAF (Rat Air Force) go on a secret mission to Bruges to blow up the Warfarin Factory on the Rühr.

Wing Commander "Ratty" Rattington-Smith (voiced by Johnny Depp) leads the band of misfits against the might of chief nasty Adolf Catler (voiced by Sir Ian McKellan). Watch out for sexy rodent Nurse Rata Hayworth (voiced by Cameron Diaz) taking on the Celia Johnstone role.

Eye-rating (geddit!): Cheesy.

NEW BRITISH CAROLS

I saw no ships
Come sailing by,
Come sailing by,
Come sailing by,
I saw no ships
Come sailing by,
Because they've all
Been axed in the
Defence cuts.

ROYAL VARIETY SHOW

And what do you do?

I'm a moron, Ma'am

"He followed me all the way home, Mum, can I keep him?"

Lines Written On The Imprisonment Of Lord Black Of Crossharbour

By William Rees-McGonagall

'Twas nearly in the year two thousand and eight
That Lord Conrad Black learned at last of his fate.
Said Amy the Judge, amidst many loud cheers.
You will go to prison for six and a half years.

The crowd all applauded this draconian sentence
Which was given because Lord Black had shown no sign of repentance.
Only from one person came the sound of boos –
It was his wife Barbara wearing one of her many pairs of shoes.

So ended the career of the great Canadian tycoon.
Whose mighty empire had come crashing doon.
Said the judge to the errant British Lord,
"You've been found guilty of 'a most wicked fraud'."

Who could have foreseen such a tragic end,
To the career of someone who had once been Mrs Thatcher's friend.
The press baron from Toronto had burst upon the English scene
Where he quickly met everyone, including Her Majesty the Queen.

The great and the good flocked to his lavish receptions,
Quite unaware of their host's shady financial deceptions.
The world all gasped at his astonishing wealth,
Little realising that he had acquired it by dishonest stealth.

Jewellery, jets and houses – nothing seemed beyond his reach.
Not even a 50-room mansion in Florida's Palm Beach.
Conrad and Barbara did nothing by half.
They even acquired London's mighty *Daily Telegraph*.

Black was now one of the great figures of the age,
Bestriding like a colossus the social and political stage.
Appropriately he moved his papers into Canary Wharf,
A tower so high that the rest of London it did dwarf.

But he needed even more money to pay for his extravagant life,
Not to mention the shopping habits of his extravagant wife.
And so Lord Black became more and more rash
As he helped himself to his shareholders' cash.

To pay for the furs and the shoes and the Bollinger
He stole from the unsuspecting shareholders of Hollinger.
Until one day these honest US investors began to complain
Saying, "Goddammit, it's us that's paying for that guy's champagne!"

But Lord Black looked down his nose at them with an arrogant sneer,
Saying "You can't touch me, I'm a British peer."
Alas, for Lord Black, in his argument there was a flaw
And soon the Chicago cops came knocking at his door.

"We've come to give you your comeuppance.
For what you have stolen is considerably more than tuppence."
And so to cut a long and sorry story short
That's how Conrad ended up in court.

Right to the end, however, he insisted he had done no wrong,
Which is why his prison sentence turned out to be so long.
And despite the entreaties of Lord Rees-Mogg and Sir Elton John
Behind bars this arrogant fat crook has finally gone.

HELP! I'VE BEEN BRUEGELED!

Ten to watch in 2008

by Phil Space

The Eye's guide to the up-and-coming stars of tomorrow

FILM Foxella Fox, 23, known as 'Foxy'. Already acclaimed by critics for her cameo as the stripper in BBC's new adaption of *Mansfield Park*. Currently in Hollywood filming action picture *Bushwacker 3* with Johnny Depp.

BOOKS Winona Hatterjii, 19. Still at Cambridge, student Winona's novella *Shooting Up* has been bought by Bloomsbury's top talent spotter Anoushka Babouska who says, "Winona's

account of the Chinese West African heroin community is a breath-taking *tour de force* which is bound to be shortlisted for the Booker Prize."

MUSIC Phukka, 19, (real name Mathew Wemyss). Rap artist Phukka has burst onto the scene with the most downloaded track of 2007, *Phukkaoff!* Originally at Charterhouse with fellow Old Carthusians, Schhit (Simon St. Clair-Grant), Wankah (Justin FotheringtonSmythe) and Respeck (Tristan de la Warr-ffrench), Phukka's fusion of hardcore dirt track and urban filtertip will make him the most sought-after act until January 31st 2008.

ART Milly Wainwright, 19. Although only six months into her art school course, Milly has quite literally set the art world alight with her self-combustible artefacts. Said curator Sir Nicholas Arsota, "The point of these works is you never know when they are going to catch fire. It could be at any moment, which is very exciting."

SPORT Tariq Aswad, 17. Hull City's No.2 keeper is already looking like Fabio Cappelo's number one choice for England goalie. Aswad has kept a clean sheet for the 5 minutes he came on against Scunthorpe in November 2007.

FASHION Yakimota Tamagotchi, 25, handpicked by Bianco Fratelli to head up his new London-based flagship label *Tutti Frutti*. 'Yaki' promises that her Spring collection will be an exciting blend of East and North.

TV Kirsty McSpangle, 21, currently fronting BBC Grampian's *Hullo Grampians*, is hotly tipped to take over as Sky's chief newsreader on the coveted 3am slot when veteran Geoff Baldie, 36, hangs up his earpiece in April.

FOOD Rick Chutney, 26, has been hailed by *Food and Foodmen* magazine as 'the most innovative newcomer to the cuisine scene in the last 3 weeks'. His new restaurant *Chutneys*, offering a range of 547 different chutneys from all over Britain, has already been closed by Health and Safety officers from Harringey's go-ahead borough council.

JOURNALISM Phillipa Space, 17, daughter of veteran journalist Phil Space who has already made her mark by compiling the above list from all the other lists printed in newspapers over the holiday period *(cont. p. 94)*.

LATE NEWS

NEW-LOOK AMBULANCES

NHS BOSSES have defended plans to replace traditional ambulances manned by a two-man crew with solo response vehicles known as 'hearses'.

"In a wide variety of emergency call-outs, these hearses, which are manned by one highly-trained funeral director, save the NHS vast sums of money, as they ensure that the patient doesn't enter the hospital system," said an NHS *(cont. p. 94)*

"Can't stop... I've got Doris on the paraglider"

'WE WON'T TREAT YOU IF YOU'RE ILL' SAYS NHS

by Our Medical Staff **C. Difficile**

ONLY PEOPLE who are 100 per cent fit will in future qualify for treatment under the National Health Service, health chiefs warned yesterday.

"We cannot be expected to treat people who have made no effort to keep themselves well," said the Government's new "fitness czar" Bob Dunkwell, formerly the chief executive of United Biscuits.

"Let's be honest, people who get ill have only got themselves to blame – treatment nowadays is very expensive and we cannot afford to waste it on people who aren't well.

"Those who are absolutely healthy must be given top priority," he concluded.

On other pages

MADDIE – NEW SIGHTING

"I'M SURE it was her," said Mrs Doris Bonkers, 69.

"I opened the paper and there she was. It was definitely her unless it was someone else." – *full story page 2.*

Sensational Diana Letter Presented To Inquiry

Drama at inquest Day 994

THERE WERE gasps of amazement when Sir Michael Mansfee QC presented the jury with an intimate letter written by the late Princess of Wales only a few days after she died.

The letter was written to Dodi in the most affectionate terms and revealed that they had been secretly married for years.

The hearing continues...

That Letter In Full

KENSINGTON PALACE

My darling fuggin Dodi, you are a fuggin' good looking guy just like your Dad and I'm going to have your fuggin' baby King Mohammed the fuggin' First of England. By the way Harrods is a fuggin' great place to shop!
your loving wife
Diana Al Fayed
signed in her absence

BURRELL EVIDENCE

Dr Hasnat Khan stole Diana's heart...

...I don't know how it ended up in my flat

'I Salute These Geniuses'

Says Max Hastings

IT IS not often in one's lifetime that one can honestly say that one has been present at an epoch-making event.

But last Sunday, as I sat in a stadium along with three million other hard-core Led Zep fans, there was no doubt in my mind that I was watching history in the making.

They are older now of course than their photographs on my treasured album covers yet the years have dealt lightly with Messrs Plant, Page *et al* and their brilliance is undimmed.

From the opening riff of the legendary Whole Lotta Love to the final exuberant chords of Stairway To Heaven, we were all enraptured by this apotheosis of rock 'n roll, the like of which the word has even known.

Even such luminaries as the Rolling Stones, Pink Floyd and even the Beatles themselves pale into insignificance beside these titans of the electric guitar.

Let me say simply this. They rocked. And I wept.

© Max Hastings, Mat D'Ancona and everyone else, 2007.

THOMAS THE TANK ENGINE

BY THE REV. TAWDRY

Part 94. Chaos at Christmas

THOMAS and all the other engines are in the shed. "We won't be needing you lot," said the Fat Controller. "It's holiday time, when everyone wants to travel, so we've shut down the network."

Thomas looked glum. "So will we be back at work for the New Year?" he asked.

"Oh no," laughed the Fat Controller. "That's when we're going to do big repair works."

Two days later, Thomas and his friends were still stuck in the shed.

"What's happened now?" asked Thomas.

"Our repairs have over-run," laughed the Fat Controller. "So you'll have a few more days off. And then, with any luck, there'll be snow so we won't have to do anything."

"But why are you so happy?" Asked Thomas. "Won't they fine you millions of pounds for the late repairs?'

"Oh yes," chuckled the Fat Controller, "but that doesn't worry us. We'll simply put the fares up to pay for the fines."

The Fat Controller was then driven home in his big shiny car to celebrate being given a knighthood in the New Year's Honours List and a suitably *fat* bonus!

The End

SCARY SPICE   SCARY SPICE   SCARY SPICE   SCARY SPICE   SCARY SPICE

Those Reunited Spice Girls

HERE'S AN "INTERESTING" QUESTION FROM A FAN ON THE WEB, SIR...

DO YOU SING YOUR OWN SONGS IN THE SHOWER?

PEOPLE ASK THE WEIRDEST THINGS, DON'T THEY?

THEY SURE DO. WHAT SHALL I REPLY?

OF COURSE I DON'T SING MY OWN SONGS IN THE SHOWER...

I HAVE MY BUTLER SING THEM FOR ME.

SOMEONE WAS TELLING ME THAT SOME CAR INSURANCE COMPANY NOW CLASSIFIES 'CELEBRITY' AS A JOB.

REALLY?

SO MANY ORDINARY PEOPLE ARE BECOMING FAMOUS THROUGH REALITY TV, THEY'VE CLASSIFIED IT AS AN OCCUPATION FOR INSURANCE RISK...

CELEBRITY AS AN OCCUPATION, EH? WHAT A WEIRD AND WONDERFUL WORLD WE LIVE IN... I CAN'T BELIEVE IT...

YOU'VE GOT A JOB!

THANKS DAD!

PAT

SHAKE

BACK IN A MO...

OH NO!.. EVER SINCE THE SMOKING BAN IT'S ALWAYS THE SAME WHEN WE GO OUT...

YOU DON'T REALLY NEED A CIGARETTE, DEBS...

YES I DO.

YOU'RE JUST FEEDING YOUR PSYCHO-LOGICAL CRAVING... YOU DON'T EVEN ENJOY SMOKING... YOU'RE JUST USING THIS AS A PROP...

YOU DON'T EVEN INHALE, DEBS...

YES, BUT I DON'T WANT THE PAPS TO REALISE I ONLY GO OUTSIDE THE CLUB TO BE SNAPPED, DO I?

OH WELL... OFF YOU GO THEN..

DAD WAS AWFULLY PROUD OF THE GREAT DEAL HE GOT FROM THE COSMETIC SURGEON.

WAS HE?

YES...

THEN I TOLD HIM I DIDN'T THINK THEY'D DONE A VERY GOOD JOB AND HE WAS GOING TO LIVE TO REGRET IT.

OH DEAR...

SO WHAT DID HE SAY?

NOTHING...BUT HIS FACE FELL...

THE STAPLES BEHIND HIS EARS HAD WORKED LOOSE APPARENTLY...

SERVE HIM RIGHT FOR BEING A CHEAPSKATE...

HOW TO CUT THROUGH RED TAPE

Those government guidelines in full

1. Pick up scissors.
2. Refer to Health and Safety Guidelines for the use of scissors, with particular reference to section 13(b) *Holding Scissors At The Correct End To Prevent Accidental Personal Harm*.
3. Go on two week Government Approved Training Course to learn correct *Scissor Procedure In The Workplace* and obtain Certificate of Scissor Handling Practice (Level 2).
4. Fill in insurance documentation including photocopy of certificate in order to ensure full cover in the event of scissor-related injury and/or cost of legal claims on behalf of Red Tape industry against scissor operatives.
5. Put down scissors.
6. Give up.

THE DAILY MYTH

Friday, 25 January 2008

FLOODS HIT ATLANTIS

by Our Weather Staff **Michael Fish**

THERE was widespread criticism of the government's building policy last night, as the city of Atlantis was lost beneath the waves for ever.

Said one Atlantian, "Why were the developers allowed to build Atlantis under the sea? Questions need to be asked and whoever is responsible should glug... glug... glug..."

On other pages
Your Rains Tonight **2**
Trident to be Replaced **3**
"We're moving to Pompeii," say couple **94**

EYE QUIZ

Spot The Balls Competition

Simply place an X where you think *(Yes, we get the picture. Ed.)*

Pinter Sells Papers To Nation For £1 Billion

by Our Heritage Staff **Professor Norman Stonehenge**

IN WHAT was described as "the literary coup of the century", the British Library has paid £1 billion for a box of old pieces of paper from Sir Harold Pinter's attic.

Among the priceless manuscripts included in this unique literary collection is a letter which will help future scholars to understand how the Nobel prizewinning playwright managed to get so much money for his archive.

The Priceless Pinter Manuscript

To the Director of the British Library

I am giving you a once-in-a-lifetime opportunity to acquire a priceless heritage item for your collection, at the giveaway price of a mere £1 billion.

Among the highly important memorabilia contained in this very wonderful archive are the following items:

1 note to milkman reading "Two pints please, chum".

1 draft of letter to President Bush beginning "You fucking warmongering bastard".

1 scorecard Surrey v. Lancashire at the Oval, July 16, 1955 (second day) signed by a member of the ground staff.

1 love letter in the author's own hand to Lady Magnesia Freelove (later Lady Pinter). Contains adult material.

Plus assorted paperclips, biro refills and other valuable literary miscellanea.

You would be mad, chummie, not to snap up this bargain offer of the millennium, which might otherwise have to go to the University of New Dworkin, Mass.

So act quickly and send your cheque by return of post.

Yours faithfully,
Sir Harold Pinter OM.

"I think we've made a real breakthrough today"

AUSTEN ADAPTATION WOWS PUBLIC

by Our Media Staff **Colonel Russell Brandon**

YES! Jane Austen has done it again with her usual trick of taking out all the sex from Andrew Davies's raunchy love romp and turning it into a polite comedy of manners.

Austen maintains that, "Beneath the obvious erotic surface of Davies's *Sex and Sexability* there is a society heaving with bonnets, carriages and card games".

"Why shouldn't I miss out a few sex scenes and shove in a quadrille or two?" Jane protested. "I mean just because it's the 18th century doesn't mean they didn't like a good dance?"

Critics, however, have accused Austen of cynically stripping out the essentials of Davies's classic bonkfest in the hope of appealing to a literary audience.

"She is just out to get readers," said TV's Mark Lawson, "It's pathetic and obvious."

Jane Austen is 191.

BLAIR CONFESSION

Forgive me Father, for I have spinned

How Democracy Works

Pt. 94
The Indo-Pakistani model

1. Inherit leadership of pro-democracy party from dead father/mother.
2. Be assassinated.
3. Pass on leadership of pro-democracy party to son/daughter.
4. Repeat process ad nauseam.

Pt. 95
The US model

1. Become president.
2. Pass on job to idiot son

(That's enough democracy, Ed.)

The Benazir I knew

by A.L.L. Hax

IN THE Oxford of the 1970s there was no more familiar or beautiful face than that of the young Benazir Bhutto, or "Booty" as she was known to her intimate group of party-going friends!

Who could resist her warm smile, her dark eyes and her winning combination of girlie confidence and serious political ambition?

Punting on the Isis, waltzing at May Balls, cycling down the high street... it is just a pity I never met her.

© *All newspapers.*

GLENDA SLAGG

FLEET STREET'S RE-TOX QUEEN!!?

■ **OOH-LA-LA!** Chapeaux off to French Monsieur Romeo – it's Nicolas Sarkozy I'm talking about, stoopid!?! Sexy Sarko's got the Gallic guts to say *au revoir* to his moaning missus and shack up with top teenage Eyetie totty Carla Bruni!!?! Can you imagine our Gordon ditching Sensible Sarah and running off with cokehead Kate Moss?!? No way José!?!? And aren't we all the poorer for it!?!! So I say trois cheers for Naughty Nicolas!?! Or Knickerless!?! (Geddit?!?)

■ **SARKOZY** – what a disgrace!?!! Calls himself the President of France but can't keep his pantalons on for long enough to run the country!?! Booh-la-la to this snail-guzzling sex maniac and his latest underage model from the land of raunchy ravioli and sex-packed spaghetti!?! You're making a fool of yourself, Nicolas, a-rumpin' and a-pumpin' with this second-hand model!?! (Geddit?!) You're not Carla's première and you won't be the dernière!?!!

So thank God says *moi* for Ungarlicky Gordon and Sober Sarah – doesn't it make you proud to be British?!?

■ *BRITNEY SPEARS* – aren'tcha-sickof her?!? Why do we have to read about every little thing she does?!? Who cares if she shaves her head!?! Who cares if she goes into the funny farm?!? Who cares if her kids are taken into care?!?? Who cares if she dies horribly!?! We do because then we won't have anything to write about. So shed a tear for sad Britney who deserves our sympathy as she shaves her head, goes into rehab and has her kids taken away from her. God bless you, Britney!?! We love ya!?!

■ HERE THEY ARE – Glenda's Winter Warmers!?!

● **Fabio Capello.** When you've finished with the English team, Fabby, how about licking *me* into shape!?!!

● **Pervez Musharraf.** Pakistan's sexy supremo – you get my vote even if there's no election!?!

● **Jacob Zuma** – the new leader of South Africa's ANC!?! OK, you're accused of money-laundering, racketeering and rape!? Why not Zuma-round to my place, Big Boy, and bring your Zulu spear with you!??!

Byeee!

ATHLETES TAKE VIAGRA SHOCK

"I hope that's a baton!"

NEWS AT TEN

SFX: Bong!
Sir Trevor McDonald: News at Ten is back.

SFX: Bong!
Fruity woman: Fruity woman brought in to look fruity.
SFX: Bong!
Sir Trevor: Sir Trevor McDonald tumbles... sorry stumbles... over his words...
SFX: Bong!
Fruity woman: Viewers turn over back to BBC News.
SFX: Bong!
Sir Trevor: And finally... News at Ten to be axed and replaced by terrible old Bond film.
SFX: Bond!
Blofeld *(for it is he)*: Ah, Mr Bong, I've been expecting you *(continues until "Carling Cup Highlights at 12.10am)*

RED NEWT THREATENED – SCIENTISTS WARN

by Our Environment Staff **Breakfast Time O'Booze**

THE rare Red Newt (*Salamander glenfiddichus*) may soon be extinct, scientists warned last night.

The newt likes to swim in a sea of whisky, but in the modern world it is becoming increasingly difficult for the newt to get away with this.

Newt watchers are desperately concerned that the last remaining Red Newt, currently to be found in the corridors of City Hall, may disappear completely under a tide of sleaze.

But some conservationists believe it is too late to save the Red Newt, saying that he should be left to die and then placed in the Natural Pissedory Museum in Red Kensington.

The New Compulsory Government Donor Card

DONOR CARD

I hereby agree in the event of my death that all my money shall be extracted from my bank account and donated to the Labour Party in order to save its life.

Signed

Home Office announcement
Carry this card with you at all times. Failure to do so will result in your arrest and a fine equivalent to all your money.

T HERE'S no other word for it. It's a complete disaster. The horrific scenes coming out of Kenya can only mean one thing. We're probably going to have to cancel our safari.

I know, it's too ghastly to contemplate, especially since I bought a new bush wardrobe and the useless Simon has bought a very expensive new camera just for the trip! Plus, we've already booked toddler Charlie into the Fun Lodge Toddler Hotel in Newbury (24-hour childcare for up to a month!!), so that we can enjoy two weeks of five-star, stress-free spa 'n' safari experience, courtesy of Excess Traveller Magazine!

And the situation is getting

POLLY FILLER

On the situation in Kenya

worse – the violence is already out of hand, as I kicked the door to the utility room very hard when I heard the latest news from Nairobi on Radio 2!! And the instability is increasing – Simon was really ratty yesterday, even when he was watching Richard Hammond's World of Jeremy Clarkson on UK Dave More Plus One.

H ONESTLY! Where is it all going to end? Surely we're not going to have to slum it in Morocco again? Or Dubai? The whole thing is a nightmare and one can only pray for peace and reconciliation to return to this benighted country in time for our connecting flight from Heathrow.

© *Polly Filler.*

Numero 94

Le Top Level Statesmanship – Blair et Sarko

Monsieur Blair (*pour c'est lui*): Bonjour Sarko – vous êtes le 'Roi de Legover', n'est-ce pas?

Monsieur Sarkozy: Bien sur – vraiment cinq fois dans la nuit – just comme vous et Cherie. J'ai read it dans le Soleil de Monsieur Murdoch.

Blair: Oui, oui, mais vous êtes too kind – votre Mademoiselle Bruni est un vrai scorcher! Ooh la la! Phwoar! Est-ce que c'est chaud in here – or est-ce que c'est moi!

Sarko: Quand vous êtes President d'Europe vous pouvez ditcher votre wife et run off avec la totty formidable tout comme moi! Marquez mes words, mon brave! C'est le futur! Sexy Sarko et Testeroni Tony! Le Ticket de Rêve!

Blair: C'est un deal!! Comptez-moi in!!

© *Kilometres Kington*

PRODUCT RECALL

The recent recruitment advertisement for the army has been withdrawn following complaints from the Health and Safety Executive that they failed to make clear that joining the army posed a genuine risk to the recruits' wellbeing. In future the advertisement will be required to read "Don't join the army as it could lead to bullying, post-traumatic stress disorder or even a severe loss of life".

BORIS MEETS CABBIES

"Keep your right-wing views to yourself, guv"

"Good news. We've discovered that you are in fact a member of the potato family"

— PILBROW —

THAT NEW HOME OFFICE PHRASEBOOK
What You Will Read

by **Polly Tickly-Correct**

THE Home Office has issued a new phrasebook to be used by police and civil servants, which it hopes will persuade the Muslim community that it is not being targeted over acts of Islamic fundamentalist terrorism.

In fact, the phrase *"acts of Islamic fundamentalist terrorism"* will be replaced by the words *"unpleasant incidents caused by nasty people"*.

Other phrases to be banned include *"Suicide bombers"* which becomes *"unfortunate cases of Extreme Self Harm"*, *"Jihad"* which becomes *"Need for greater understanding of different faiths"* and *"7/7"*, which becomes *"25/12"* or *"Christmas"*.

● Full story plus pix **94**

NEW IN THE EYE
ME AND MY PANTS
THIS WEEK

JEREMY PAXMAN

Are pants important to you?

That's a bloody stupid question.

Do you have a favourite pair of pants?

Oh come off it…

Boxers or y-fronts?

None of your bloody business.

Do you think Marks and Spencer's underwear is… *pants*?

Look, let's get this absolutely right: it was a personal e-mail about a purely private matter, OK?

So how did it… *get out*?

Are you trying to be funny?

No, I'm being… *supportive*.

Right. I've had enough of this. (At this point Mr Paxman ripped off his microphone and stormed out. As a result, we were unable to ask the traditional question, "Has anything amusing ever happened to you in relation to your pants?")

NEXT WEEK: *Sir Herbert Gusset "Me And My Gusset".*

BLAIR RECEIVED INTO BANK WITH SIMPLE CEREMONY

by Our Religious Affairs Correspondent **Phil Wallet**

TONY BLAIR was today formally received into the J.P. Morgan Bank in New York.

In a simple but moving ceremony, the former prime minister was blessed by the bank's chairman Mr J.P. Mammonburger III, attended by members of the board robed in their traditional dark suits and sober ties.

Said Mr Blair afterwards, "For me this is the fulfilment of a lifelong journey. I have always believed in money, but obviously so long as I was prime minister I couldn't admit this publicly, even though my wife Cherie was known to be a devout cashaholic."

Nicene Greed

"In Britain," Mr Blair went on, "people become embarrassed if you talk too openly about believing in money."

"As my friend Mr Campbell used to say, 'we don't do money'."

"But, now I'm no longer in office, I can speak openly about what it means to me – which is everything!"

"I will admit," he confessed,

"that there have been many dark times when the only thing that sustained me was my faith in money and the belief that one day I would have lots of it."

Wages of Spin

A spokesman for the bank said that they were delighted to welcome, "this new worshipper into the fold."

"People come to us through many different paths, but they are all united in the one true faith – and today we were all thrilled to see Tony being given his first cheque for $2 million, as a sign that he had been received into full communion with the great brotherhood of rich people throughout the world."

IN THE COURTS

'I'm No Bugger,' Says Fugger

Day 94: *Inquest into the death of Diana, the Late Princess of Wales (Fugger v. The Truth)*

"Murder? You do realise that if you do that again you'll be in serious trouble young man!"

THE INQUEST resumed today before Mr Justice Scott-Carrot, when the sister of the deceased, Lady Sabrina McCorkscrew, told the court of her last conversations with her sister.

Philip Chequetrouser QC *(on behalf of the Metropolitan Police, Tesco supermarkets and the Council for the Protection of Rural England):* Lady Sabrina, would you kindly tell the court what the late St Diana said when she rang you from the jacuzzi deck on board Mr Fayed's yacht, the Flying Fugger, on the night of August 28th 1997?

Lady Sabrina: Yah. She said, "You'd better be careful what you say, Sabby, because you-know-who has bugged the phone."

Sir Michael Hugefee QC *(for the plaintiff Mr Al-Fugger):* Is this not clearly a reference to the Duke of Edinburgh, acting in collaboration with MI6, whose agents are supremely well-versed in the dark arts of surveillance and secret espionage?

Fayed: Too fuggin' right! You tell him like it is, Hugefee. That's what I'm fuggin' paying you for.

Lady Sabrina: Are you thick or what? I'm talking about you, Mr Fayed. She thought you were listening in to everything she said.

Fayed: Are you calling me a fuggin' bugger? I tell you, Mohammed is no shirtlifter. Not like the fuggin' Duke of Edinburgh, with his pooftah kilt.

Scottlecarrot: Mr Fayed, you appear to be the victim of a linguistic misunderstanding, perhaps due to your foreign origins. The word "bugger" can refer to two distinct types of activity, only one of which is still illegal, more's the pity you may think, though that is a matter for you. On the one hand, it may refer to two consenting adults in the privacy of a public convenience of their choice. On the other, it may describe the privy fixing of an unobtrusive electronic device, to enable a third party to overhear the conversations, on the telephone or otherwise, of those parties whose intercourse has thus been illicitly trespassed upon.

Chequetrouser: Your Lordship has put the matter very succinctly, if I may say so.

Scott-Carrot: I am indebted to you.

Lady Sabrina: Can someone tell me what's going on here? I've got a very important hairdressing appointment with Jean-Claude at 3.30 and I really can't afford to miss it.

Scott-Carrot: I quite understand your predicament, Lady McCorkscrew, and I must apologise for wasting your time, but I am sure you will understand that we must spin things out for as long as we can here, so that the entire legal profession can continue in gainful employment for many years to come.

(The case continues...)

"Nutcase dismissed!"

End of Diana Inquest

POLICE LOG

Neasden Central Police Station

Office hours: 9-12 Mon-Tues (except Tuesday)

0937 hrs Armed Response Unit sent to Neasden Market after Trading Standards Officer Tim Grott reported a fruit and vegetable merchant using the outlawed Imperial unit "pounds" in a commercial transaction. The trader, Ms Prunehat, resisted arrest, even after admitting that she had used the phrase "That'll be two pounds thirty-five" as she handed over the assorted comestibles. She was subdued by Taser and charged under EU Directive 373A(ii) Section 42.

1053 hrs Ansaphone message received from Neasden Magistrates Court alerting officers to the release on bail of a gang of five youths charged with murder. The youths were granted bail on condition that they didn't murder the same person again. They all promised the court that they would abide by this restriction. Recorded reply assures "Your call is important to us."

1104 hrs Ansaphone message received from member of public claiming that five youths now drunk and heading for Herbert Morrison Estate. Recorded reply informs "Your call is still important to us" and directs caller to the Support The Police Pay Rise website at www.knackercash.co.uk.

No further entries were recorded in the log due to redeployment of all officers in preparing paperwork for important case, *Regina et EU vs Prunehat*. Ms Prunehat, for the record, has been refused bail.

Gnome

READERS of my newspapers will be sickened by the recent stories of MPs giving jobs to their wives and families regardless of their ability. This is nepotism pure and simple and an affront to the cherished traditions of meritocracy that have made this country the envy of the world.

We are all of one mind here at Gnomes International in unreservedly condemning this sleazy preferment of relatives which has tarnished the reputation of the Mother of Parliament.

LORD GNOME
(Chairman, Gnomes International)

HON. JIMMY GNOME
(CEO, Gnome Communications)

HON. LAKELAND GNOME
(Gnome Retail plc)

HON. LIZZY GNOME
(Managing Director, GnomeSat TV)

LADY WENDY GNOME
(President, Gnome China Corp)

MS RITA CHEVROLET
(Research Assistant and Massage Coordinator)

GNOME INTERNATIONAL
LONDON – NEW YORK – PEKING – DIGGER'S ROCK

CONWAY FAMILY VALUES

If they paid me more money, I wouldn't have to be so greedy

My father is as straight as I am

He's a proper Tory MP. He's sleeping with his secretary

Dad's got the sack – and it's full of money

SLEAZY COME – SLEAZY GO!

New Words

Administrative shortcomings *(n. compound)* theft, particularly from public funds. Example: "Mr Derek Conway has repeatedly committed acts of administrative shortcomings by giving huge sums of taxpayers' money to members of his family" (Hansard, 2008).

Research assistant *(n.)* personal relative who receives large sums of public money in return for doing nothing. Example: "Another bottle of Dom Perignon for Mr Conway's research assistant" (overheard in University bar, 2007), or "I was at school with both of Mr Conway's research assistants" (F. Wheen, Old Harrovian Newsletter, 2008).

Secretary *(n.)* wife. Example: "Who was that secretary I saw you with last night?" "That was no secretary, that was my wife." (Old Parliamentary Jokes No. 94)

Conway *(n.)* slang variant for conman, fraudster, one who embezzles public funds.

TWO BOYS RELATED TO NATIONAL PUBLIC FIGURE PAID BY THE TAXPAYER TO DO NOTHNG WHO SPEND ALL THEIR TIME IN NIGHT CLUBS

SPEAKER ON SLEAZE

Order! Order! Order a taxi for my wife!

"I'm disillusioned with the government…"

"That's nothing. I'm disillusioned with the next one…"

"Today, I want to speak to you all about this country's moral vacuum"

Exclusive to the Daily Mail

The True Story Of Why Blair Backed Bush – Was It Cash For War?

asks award-winning columnist STEPHEN GLOVE

FOR FIVE years it has been the greatest mystery of British politics – why did Tony Blair give such unequivocal support to President Bush's mad and ill-fated invasion of Iraq?

Among the many possible explanations for this extraordinary decision is the improbable suggestion that the prime minister only backed Bush in the hope of cashing in on lucrative American deals on his eventual retirement.

Let me be clear. Not for a moment am I accusing Mr Blair of being so greedy for money and so devoid of conscience that he would be prepared to risk the lives of thousands of British servicemen in exchange for millions of dollars paid by US publishers, bankers, insurance companies and lecture circuits.

Yet, when you observe Mr Blair's behaviour since leaving office, as he desperately attempts to pay off the vast mortgages on his various reckless property deals, one cannot help but see the former prime minister in a new light.

Let me say again, for the benefit of the lawyer who is sitting beside me as I type these words, that I am not for a minute claiming that Mr Blair only supported President Bush in order to fill his boots with blood money.

Such a wild allegation would be outrageous, even if it were true, which it is not.

All the same, the facts speak for themselves. What seems to be now emerging is *(Cont. p. 94)*

● *TOMORROW: Did Tony only sign the EU Treaty as part of a secret deal with Sarkozy and Merkel to make him EU President?* (No. Mail lawyer.)

The 2008 Hugh Cudlipp Memorial Lecture In Full

The Role of the Media In Contemporary Britain

by Alastair Campbell

Good evening, scumbags. I'll tell you what's wrong with the media nowadays. They're so pathetic that they believed all those lies I told them. Ha, ha, ha. Can I have my fucking cheque, please? © A. Campbell

THE NEW DWORKIN BEE

Friday 8 February, 2008

LONDON MAYORAL PRIMARIES
Crowds go wild for Borik Obarmy

by Our UK correspondent **Hiram J Pipesucker II**

LARGE NUMBERS of enthusiastic Londoners are responding to the charisma of a new phenomenon that is sweeping London's political scene like a tornado.

Borik Obarmy looks set to become the first Turkish mayor of the city of London in a historic election victory later this year.

His supporters say that Borik is like a breath of fresh air with his youthful good looks and his appeal to women everywhere.

Maybe Borik *is* short on specific policies but he is long on charm.

Alas Poor Borik

Said veteran UK commentator Lord Rees Mogg, "He reminds me of the young Charles Kennedy before he was assassinated by Ming Campbell."

One thing is for sure: Borik stands for change and change is the one thing Londoners crave.

ON OTHER PAGES
● "I witness the Borik Magic", by Andrew Gimson   p2
● "Will Borik get the black vote?" Leader p3
● Borik's wife: is she his secret weapon?   p94

CRIME SHOCK
Survey Of Male Teenagers – Results In Full

● 99% have been "involved in crime"
● 100% "not there when it happened"
● 110% "good in knife fights"
● 120% "not virgins"
● 0% "gay"

"An' the big blade is for killin' people"

KING FUG GOES ON SHOW

by Our Legal Staff **Howard Carter-Fuck**

MILLIONS queued today outside the Law Courts to see the fabled 'King Fug', on show for the first time in London.

The legendary King Fugginarshole – to give him his full Egyptian name – is over 83 years old but still manages to cast a hypnotic spell over subsequent generations with his immortal curse, "It was the fuggin' Duke of Edinburgh, MI6 and the fuggin' Loch Ness Monster."

Fiat Justitia

Rivals who suffered from the "Curse of Fug" included African potentate "Tiny" M'Rowland, who died in mysterious circumstances at the age of 96 when stung by a mysterious Egyptian wasp when travelling in Uganda. *(Is this right? Ed.)*

In his palace at Harrods, King 'Fug' held sway with a court of toadying eunuchs led by the Chief Bouffant, Mike al-Cole, who attended his master's every whim with a loyalty and devotion unparalleled in human history.

In De Nile

Legend has it that young handmaidens quailed as King Fug approached them for "favours" as they toiled slicing bacon in the Food Hall.

But, in spite of his opulence and wealth, King Fug feared for his own life and surrounded himself with bodyguards who were usually drunk and were unsafe when put in charge of the Royal Chariot – often colliding with pyramids or Cleopatra's Needles.

Henri Paul-Bearer

One exhibit bound to be popular with visitors is the mile-high pile of gold which King Fug gave to his trusty lawyer, Mike al-Manservant, in exchange for telling lies before the Supreme Judges.

But undoubtedly the highlight of this exhibition will be the death mask of King Fug himself, the image of the Bore King which is one of the supreme wonders of the world and which *(cont. p. 94)*

WEDDING OF THE CENTURY

 How They Are Related

Old Nick	Brunihilda
|	|
St Nikolas	Isambard Kingdom Bruni
|	|
Czar Nicholas the Randy	Mickey Brooni
|	|
The Dame of Sarkozy	Wayne Bruni
|	|
Nicholas Soamesy	Bruni The Bare
|	|
Sarko Marx	Karl Marx
|	|
Sarki (H.H. Munro)	Carl Orff
|	|
Sarkozy Fan Tutti	Carla Kitorff
|	|
Nicholas Teacozy	**Carla Nudi**

"Do you do abortions?"

POLICE LOG

Neasden Central Police Station
Office hours: 9-5.30pm Mon-Tues (except Tuesday)

8 February 2008

0900 hrs All officers assigned to form-filling duties.

1100 hrs Officers continue with form-filling duties.

1300 hrs Break for lunch, all officers fill in 94-page 'Lunch Evaluation Assessment Form'.

1500 hrs Form-filling duties continue.

1700 hrs Duty Officer checks station ansaphone. Member of public reports Romanian child trafficking gang openly conducting prostitute slave auction in Tesco car park opposite police station. No officers are available to respond, due to higher-priority initiatives, ie form-filling.

1715 hrs Further form-filling duties including 940-page Assessment of Daily Form-Filling Target Attainment Form.

1730 hrs Station to close. Ansaphone recommends public seek advice and help on criminal or judicial matters from Neasden Sharia Court, 712 Poundstretcher Road.

VENUS GOES FOR IT!

Nationwide Fury Erupts As Archbishop 'Converts To Islam'

by Our Political Staff **The Rev. Rowan Pelling**

A STORM of anger engulfed Britain today following an unprecedented outburst from Britain's top prelate, Rowan Atkinson.

Addressing an audience of several other men with beards attending a theological conference at St Dullstan's, the Archbishop of Canterbury was speaking on the theme of "Toward Multi-Cultural Plurality in a Secular Society".

The Rev. Atkinson's astonishing references to Sharia law, Islam and the role of patio heaters in promoting global warming immediately made headlines across the world.

Off With His Beard!

The Queen herself was said to be "furious" and "deeply disturbed" at what she privately referred to as "Dr Williams's treasonable conversion to Mohammedanism".

The leaders of all three political parties were quick to condemn a speech which none of them had heard.

A Downing Street spokesman said, "The suggestion that we should erect giant cranes in London and hang people from them flies in the face of our British traditions of fair play."

A spokesman for Mr David Cameron and Mr Nick Clegg said, "We agree with every word the Prime Minister said. He is quite right to call for the Archbishop to be hanged from a crane in central London – that is the way we do things in this country."

Other church leaders joined in the wave of protests. The former Archbishop of Canterbury, Dr George Cariaandsharia, said, "I was much better at being Archbishop than him."

The Chief Imam of Tunbridge Wells, Abu Hamsa Kneesand-

bumpsemoff, said, "How dare the Archbishop suggest that Islamic law should be imposed on Britain? It is an insult to the Prophet. He should be strung up from a crane."

Stone Me!

The general public too were quick to express their outrage at the Archbishop's suggestion that all British schoolgirls should be forced to wear head-to-toe burqas or be stoned to death.

Said a typical London cab driver, summing up the nation's mood, "Blimey, guv. That Archbishop, what a twat. Those Muslims go around having eight wives – I mean, one's bad enough! Ha, ha, ha. I've just bought one of them patio heaters. Fantastic. Like a ruddy toaster in my garden now. I was sitting there in my vest last night, having a fag. That Archbishop must be off his rocker. If he thinks I'm going to stop the cab every five minutes to pray to Mecca, you'd never get wherever it was you were going. Where was it? Newton Abbot, did you say? I'll have to get one of those satnavs."

That Shock Lecture In Full – The Words That Shook The Nation

...Whilst it may be argued that some form of compromise may have to be reached, between the divergent demands of the moral and ideological traditions of the various faith-communities which co-exist in parallelity, as opposed to a hierarchical relationship whereby the secular imperative dominates to the detriment of those value-systems and prescriptions which underwrite the belief-structures integral to the major Abrahamic and indeed other non-Abrahamic world religious grapefruit segments...

STOP PRESS

Archbishop 'Says Sorry And Returns To Church of England'

In a shock clarification last night, the Archbishop of Canterbury claimed that his controversial speech had been "misunderstood" by everyone, including himself.

To a standing ovation lasting several hours, he told the General Synod, "If there has been an inadvertent unclarity with regard to my views on the grapefruit segment issue, then let me make it clear that at no point was I advocating a parallel segmentation of these fruit systems which might in due course lead to a regrettable but inevitable grapefruit-isation, as I think we have to call it, of British culture and indeed all other *(cont. p. 94)*

Thought for the Day

FROM THE ARCHBISHOP OF CANTERBURY

"And there now abideth these three – faith, hope and clarity. And the greatest of these is clarity."

Lookalikes

Marquis de Sade　　**Max Mosley**

Sir,
　The Guardian recently published pictures of these two gentlemen. Are they by any chance related?

　ENA B. SMAXWELL
　(with thanks to reader
　D.C. Manison for the tip-off).

Goody　　**Seal**

Sir,
　I was struck between the similarity between an irate Jade Goody and an elephant seal...
　DAN HAYES,
Via email.

Iggy　　**Heather**

Sir,
　I know Mr Pop often sets out to offend, but marrying a Beatle? Shurely that's going too far. It can only end in disaster.
　KATHERINE DIXON,
Via email.

Cruise　　**Barrowman**

Sir,
　Has anybody noticed the similarity in appearance between John Barrowman and Tom Cruise? One is a member of a group that fights alien conspiracies from its Torchwood HQ – the other conspires to torch all opposition from its alien HQ.
　TONY SANDY,
Via email.

Duchess　　**Shackleton**

Princess　　**Shackleton**

Sir,
　Fiona Shackleton, divorce lawyer for Paul McCartney and previously Prince Charles, underwent a very interesting metamorphosis after receiving her famous dousing by the volatile Ms Heather Mills. She arrived as the bouffant Camilla and left a tad like the wet-look Diana. Surely they must be related?
　Yours,
　LYNNE BOOTH,
Via email.

Corporal　　**Governor**

Sir,
　Dad's Army's Corporal Jones of "Don't panic, Mr Mainwaring" fame bears an uncanny resemblance to Bank of England Governor, Mervyn King of "Don't panic, Darling" fame. Are they perchance related?
　Yours,
　JANET BURKE,
Via email.

Liberace　　**Conway**

Sir,
　I couldn't help noticing the astonishing resemblance between Henry "blond, bouncy and one for the boys" Conway and another man quite happy to shell out large amounts of money to young male employees who appeared to do very little in return...
　ENA B. SEEINGYOU,
Via email.

Ego　　**Self**

Sir,
　The gloomy and terrifying restaurant critic from Ratatouille – Anton Ego (aka The Grim Eater) – and the cadaverous writer Will Self are surely related?
　Self? Ego? I rest my case.
　RODDY MURRAY,
Isle of Lewis.

Princess　　**Princess**

Sir,
　I could not help noticing an uncanny similarity between the bit-part actor Princess Beatrice (for it is she) and Princess Fiona of Shrek 1, 2 and 3 fame.
　Is there a sinister side to the Windsor dynasty? I feel we should be told.
　Yours faithfully,
　STUART MCCUBBIN,
South Gosforth, Newcastle upon Tyne.

Bean　　**Sarkozy**

Sir,
　Is there any chance the French (and EU) presidency has in fact been infiltrated by cunning agents provocateurs?
　I think we should be told (if only in mime).
　KEN TOUGH.
Vancouver, Canada.

Spector　　**Struwwelpeter**

Sir,
　Could someone look into the age of Phil Spector – could he have modelled for the Struwwelpeter character?
　Regards,
　SIMON THOMPSON,
Via email.

Cartoon character
Senior Republican

Sir,
Is it me or does John McCain look more and more like Popeye The Sailor these days?
GREGORY BRENNAN,
Liverpool.

Duke
Grendel

Sir,
Imagine my surprise to see the Duke of Edinburgh in 3D slaughtering defenceless Vikings. Are Grendel and HRH by any chance related?

LYNNE JOHNSON,
Skipton.

Bernie
Anne

Sir,
I can't help noticing the uncanny likeness between the "grieving widow" Anne Darwin and Formula One supremo Bernie Ecclestone. The jury's out on whether they share the same hairdresser, optician or are simply both having a miserable, grimacing time of late.
Yours,
KEVIN WOOLDRIDGE,
Via email.

Sipowicz
Amaral

Sir,
I wonder if any of your readers have noticed the striking resemblance between the sacked Portuguese detective Chief Inspector Gonçalo Amaral, and Detective Andy Sipowicz from "NYPD Blue"?
One was once memorably described as "a drunken, racist goon with a heart of gold". The other is less highly regarded – at least by the British press.
Yours,
ENA B. MANNORAK,
London W2.

Ken
Gibbon

Sir,
Could this be Ken Livingstone?
With the grudging compliments of
BARRY HUMPHRIES.

Sam The Eagle
Darling

Sir,
I always knew our new Chancellor was a complete and utter Muppet...
ENA B. FARRIMOND,
London W1.

Winehouse
Callas

Sir,
Check the eye make-up!
KATHRYN TURNER,
Via email.

Duke
Grendel

Sir,
I wonder if any of your readers have noticed the striking resemblance between The Hood, erstwhile bad man from the Gerry Anderson's TV series "Thunderbirds" and Adam Applegarth, Chief Executive of Northern Rock. How could a banker possibly be related to a 1960's puppet representation of a ne'er do well? I feel we should be told.
Yours sincerely,
RICHARD DORSET,
Newcastle.

Putin
Kronsteen

Sir,
From Russia with Love – has anyone noticed the resemblance between Vladimir Putin, President of the Russian Federation, and Vladek Sheybal as Kronsteen, boss of the former KGB assassination agency SMERSH? Could they by any chance share some DNA? I think we should be told.
John Rushby-Smith,
Via email.

Wilkinson
Squirrel

Sir,
An uncanny resemblance, don't you think?
Yours,
J. STEWART,
Glos.

Alien
Brand

Sir,
I love Russell Brand tremendously, but I can't help seeing the alien in him...
GILL PERKINS,
Via email.

Magoo
Fayed

Sir,
In the attached pictures your readers may notice the resemblance between Mr Magoo and Mr Fayed. One is a lovable cartoon character; the other is wearing a fez.
CATH BOYLAN,
London.

The Ballad Of Speaker Martin

By Sir William Rees-McGonagall

Now gather ye round, guid men and true
For I have a tale to tell to you.
I tell the story of Speaker Martin,
A bonnie lad frae the land of the tartan.

He was born of humble folk in Glasgie toon –
On the social scale ye couldnae gang further doon.
Barefoot wee Michael walked the cobbled streets
Until he got a job hammering metal sheets.

His fellow workers soon chose him as their leader,
Saying "Yon Mick Martin is a canny wee bleeder."
And so he became a Union boss
And for the greedy capitalists he gave ne'er a toss.

In time he was elected as a Labour MP –
Springburn was the name of his constituency.
So our Scottish hero came down to take his seat
In the Mother of Parliaments, which was no mean feat.

For years and years no one even knew his name
Let alone from whence he came.
Until one day as fate transpired
The well-loved Speaker, Betty Boothroyd, suddenly retired.

When the MPs neeeded her successor to pick
Who did they choose but the unknown Mick?
For the bemused Mr Martin it was his lucky day –
A cushy job and loads of extra pay.

So see him now, enthroned in glory.
On one side Labour, the other Tory.
With his buckled shoes and braided gown
Was there any finer sight in London town?

There he presided, shouting "Order! Order!"
This once-humble lad frae north o' the border.
But alack for the hapless Glasgie lad,
At being the Speaker he turned out to be extremely bad.

Bumbling and stumbling, he made such a mess
That it eventually caught the attention of the press.
"These slurs on my reputation are making me sick,"
Said Martin. "Why, they are calling me 'Gorbals Mick'."

"These jumped-up toffs from their public schools
Are accusing *me* of breaking Parliamentary rules.
This is just an attack on the working class.
That Quentin Letts from the *Daily Mail* can kiss my arse."

It must be admitted that Mick could be quite coarse.
He could scream profanities until his voice was hoarse.
He had even been heard to shout, "Oh f*ck!
Get me the services of libel lawyers Carter Ruck!"

But the more he protested, the deeper the hacks dug
And the smile on Mick's face became ever less smug.
Every day there came a new revelation
To shock the hard-working folk of the British nation.

Taxis to Tesco for his wife to go shopping
For items of food such as tomato pizza topping.
Free travel by air for his wife and his bairns
Worth almost as much as the average man earns.

Soon there arose a universal shout –
"It's time to throw yon auld booby out!
Of this posturing ninny, we are heartily sick.
It's time for ye to gang awa', ye ghastly Gorbals Mick!"

And so ends the tale of Speaker Martin
Who soon frae his office will be departin'.
And what is the moral of this tragic story?
They'd have been better off choosing some terrible
old Tory.

NEW STAMP OFFER

Jack Straw

Jacqui Smith

Geoff Hoon

Andy Burnham

Tessa Jowell

A NEW set of stamps was issued today by the Royal Mail to commemorate Great British Hypocrites.

The stamps depict senior ministers who are campaigning to save the post offices in their constituencies despite the Government's policy of national closures.

A spokesperson for the Royal Mail said, "You can buy these stamps at your local post office – or you probably can't."

Beijing Olympics
New Record Set

AMERICA's Stephen Spielberg today set a new Olympic record as he ran away from the Chinese Olympics in an astonishing two years.

Spielberg's time to realise that the Chinese aren't really very nice was one of the slowest since records began.

Said a Chinese spokesman, "Mr Spielberg was originally happy to take the gold, but when it turned out he was going to get the silver (30 pieces) he decided to run for it."

(Reuters)

Prince Harry
An Apology

IN COMMON with all other newspapers, we may in recent years have given the impression that we regarded Prince Harry as a drunken, useless, upperclass layabout whose single purpose in life was to hang around nightclubs, chase "totty" and indulge in loutish behaviour, often involving gentlemen of the press.

Headlines such as "Yes! It's Your Royal Lowness!", "Prince Charmless Punches Paparazzi" and "Born To Be Drunk" may have conveyed to our readers the idea that we in some way held the Prince in low esteem and viewed him as a degenerate wastrel not fit to hold a commission in Her Majesty's Armed Forces and a disgrace to his mother, St Diana of Hearts.

We now realise that there was not a jot or scintilla of truth whatsoever in any of the above. Furthermore, we now realise that Prince Harry is a role model for the nation's youth, a warrior prince in the mould of King Henry V and a credit to his country, his family and the memory of his late mother, Princess Diana of Calcutta.

Headlines from this week's press such as "Hero Harry Single-Handedly Defeats Taliban", "Welcome Home And God Bless You, Prince Valiant" and "Jordan's Knockers World's Biggest – It's Official!" have hopefully redressed any misunderstandings that may have arisen due to our earlier reports.

IN TOMORROW'S PAPER: ● *How long before Harry falls off the wagon?* 2 ● *Lock up your daughters! Harry's back!* 3 ● *What now for the layabout Prince?* 5

© All newspapers

War is Hello!

THE DAILY TELEGRAPH Friday, March 7, 2008

Letters *to the* Editor

Prince Harry's successful mission

SIR – As one of those who served on the North-West frontier and saw at first hand the White Man's Graveyard with the vultures circling overhead as our beleaguered column fought its way through the territory now controlled by Johnny Taliban (note, not "Terry", as the young officers refer to it nowadays), may I say that much as I welcome the acclaim given to the young Prince Harry for doing his duty at the sharp end, I must deplore the length of his hair and the grave failure of his senior officers to ensure that it was kept at regulation length, i.e. ¼ inch above the ears and ⅛ inch from nape to lower cranium. Had *I* come on parade in Kabul looking like a "mop-topped Beatle", I would have been on a charge and spent the rest of my career doing well-earned Field Punishment no.3, i.e. being buried up to my neck in sand and eaten alive by giant ants – the dreaded Talibants, as they were known to generations of British serving men.

Brigadier F.B.J. Newman-Gusset
The Old Tally Barn, Crewcutte, Dorset.

SIR – May I suggest a statue of Prince Harry as the ideal occupant of the empty plinth in Trafalgar Square? Perhaps the square itself should be renamed as Helmand Piazza in honour of the prince's heroic victory over the Taleban.

Rear Admiral Sir Horatio Horn-Concerto (Retired)
The Old Lighthouse, Hartley Wintney.

SIR – In his pursuit of the enemy in Helmand Province perhaps the fox-hunting prince should cry "Tally Ban Ho!".

Michael Giggler
Via email.

The Guardian Friday March 7 2008

Letters and emails

Prince Harry's failed PR stunt

It was totally sickening to read the garbage spouted by the media about Prince Harry's so-called heroic deeds, i.e. murdering innocent Muslims *viz* the popular, democratic and socially responsible Taliban freedom fighters... er... as if they were no more than pheasants on a shoot at Sandringham... er... in itself a disgraceful ritual of mass annihilation by the decadent Royal Fascist Family... er... to suggest that this gung-ho upper class representative of the reactionary military-industrial complex... er... is to be applauded is to my mind totally sickening, particularly at a time when nursery schools are being closed and local post offices are being turned into runways so that American torture flights can land and kidnap...er... Jon Snow put it so well... the really sickening conspiracy is that of the media like Channel 4 er...

Dave Spart
c/o The Back Ken Livingstone, Hang Boris Johnson Campaign, Flat 17b, Rusbridger House, Rowson Road, E94.

Is it not time that Prince Harry was charged with war crimes along with Gordon Brown, Tony "Poodle Blair" and George Bush? Would it not be only just for the prince to be hung from a crane in Baghdad after a fair trial under Sharia Law had found him guilty in the Iraqi courts?

G. Galloway MP
c/o Talk Spart Radio, London.

Surely the prince's service in Afghanistan deserves promotion. Or should that be self-promotion?

Mike Giggler
Via email.

GNOMEWORTH
Product Recall

FOLLOWING complaints, Gnomeworths is withdrawing its "Paedo" range of children's underwear. When the range was launched we were unaware of the connotations of the word "Paedo". Only when our staff looked up the word on Wikipaedophile did it emerge that "Paedo" was perhaps an unsuitable brand name for this type of merchandise. It has now been renamed "The Glitter Collection" to avoid giving further offence to our customers.

GNOMEWORTH 2008

"Please Miss! My waters have broken!"

Oscar Frocks Shocks!

By Our Resident Fashion Editor **Liz Slagg**

IT'S Oscar time again, folks, and as usual we've got our fair share of frocks that rock and dresses that depress us!

Cameron Diazz-les us with a graceful off-pink number that promises salmon-chanted evenings!

Ouch! **Camer-ingue Diaz**'s fussy frills make her look more like there's something about Meringue than Mary!

Bridget Jones's Dire-ry! Note in today's entry, **Renée**, dated shiny stuff, v. v. bad!

Renée Swell-weger, certainly keeps up with the Jones's in this stunning sparky number!

Dame, set and match to **Helen Mirren** for showing off her right royal figure

Off with her hem! This shapeless sight will have even the Queen seeing red!

(That's enough. Ed.)

Deedes Romance With The Youthful Queen Victoria

(taken from the new sensational biography *Dirty Deedes* by Robinson Jammy)

IN HIS old age, I can reveal, the legendary Fleet Street reporter William Deedes fell hopelessly in love with the young Queen Victoria.

The unlikely couple met at Royal Ascot in 1840, when the already elderly Deedes was covering the race meeting as a reporter for the now-defunct Morning Post.

"He was a sweet old gentleman," recorded the smitten Victoria in her diary that evening, "and he gave me a tip for a horse that came last."

The couple several times travelled together overseas, including an incognito visit to the front-line of the Crimean War, which Deedes was covering for the now-

defunct Daily Telegraph.

The young Victoria was captivated by Deedes's stories of how he had met William the Conqueror and played bowls with Sir Francis Drake (whom he likes to recall 'wore odd-coloured socksh').

The Prince Consort, however, took a dim view of the liaison, and on Victoria's marriage gave orders that the relationship should cease.

Deedes was heartbroken and threw himself with redoubled vigour into his work. He only outlived his former beloved by a mere 106 years.

● *In tomorrow's Daily Kissandtelegraph* **'Posh and Deedesh: How Bill Seduced Victoria Beckham'.**

Mary Ann Bighead on the platonic friendship between a brilliant writer and the late **Bill Deedes**

Bill Deedes was the most extraordinary journalist of the 20th century because he was the only one who didn't try and jump on me within seconds of our meeting!

In fact, every single male adult in British public life fancies me rotten. True! They can't help it. The Mary Ann Bighead allure drives them wild: Cabinet Ministers, Peers, Editors, Admirals of the Fleet, Archbishops of Canterbury... all go weak at the knees as soon as I appear.

But with Bill it was different. Of course he was secretly gagging for it, but being a true gentleman, he studiously and politely covered it up by refusing to flirt with me even though it was quite clear he was dying to get me into the sack – like everyone else, including the President of the United States, Professor Stephen Hawking and, on one memorable journalistic trip to EuroDisney with my daughters Brainella and Intelligencia, all *seven* of Snow White's dwarves!

So it is quite clear that Bill Deedes could never have had an affair with anyone, as this new, so-called biography claims. If he didn't try it on with me, he would obviously never have been tempted by any other woman.

Posterity may record that Bill Deedes was best known for his journalistic exploits, or for his famous appearance as "Boot" in Evelyn Waugh's *Scoop* or as the golfing partner of Denis Thatcher and recipient of the notorious "Dear Bill" letters in *Private Eye*.

But I know better, as usual.

The most remarkable achievement of the 94-year-old journalistic icon was his ability to keep his trousers on when Mary Ann Bighead was in the room!

PS. So much for those who say all I do is write about how clever I am. In this column I have just written about how sexually irresistible I happen to be. Pretty modest, eh? And clever with it.

© *Mary Ann Bighead 2008.*

here you are tramp, spend it on food, not booze and drugs

yeah, cheers mate, I'll probably get myself a rocket and parmesan salad

Daily Eye

FRIDAY, 7 MARCH, 2008

JOIN OUR CAMPAIGN TO SAVE THE PLANET BY BANNING THIS TIDAL WAVE OF DANGEROUS RUBBISH

By Our Environmental Staff
Polly Vinyl-Chloride

EVERY DAY Britons consume 2 million copies of the Daily Mail.

They are used for just a few seconds and then thrown away.

Every year that makes a rubbish mountain 14 times higher than Everest.

The entire country is now polluted with several billion tons of discarded Daily Mails, filling our streets, fields, rivers and seas with the disgusting detritus of Britain's most toxic newspaper.

From one end of the country to the other, wildlife is dying – poisoned by articles by Geoffrey Levy, Amanda Platell and Richard Littlejohn, not to mention cartoons by Mac and Mahood.

Last night top celebrities were lining up to back our campaign to clean up Britain, among them top ex-newsreader Angela Rippon, former *That's Life* star Esther Rantzen, the late Hughie Green and Tory MP David Cameron.

One of Britain's most beautiful woodlands is disfigured by millions of copies of the Daily Mail littering our once green and pleasant land

Banish The Mail

Now you too can back our campaign by signing this coupon and sending it to the Prime Minister.

Dear Prime Minister,

I would like to register my very deep concern at the environmental damage being done to Britain and the world by the Daily Mail.

Please stop sucking up to Paul Dacre and banish this horrible product forever.

Signed...............................

RUSSIAN ELECTIONS IN FULL

PUTINGRAD SOUTH

Dimitri Medvedev, The Not Putin Oh No Not Me I'm Independent Party .... **600 million**

Igor Stroganov, Neo-Stalinist Party **36**

The Late Ivana Die, People's Democratic Alliance Party..........**0**

110% swing to Putin.

SIBERIA NORTH

Oleg Dedski, United Opposition Movement............**0° Centigrade**

Nikolai Gulag, Bring Back Glasnost Coalition.............**-37°F**

Czar Putin the First (Vlad the Impaler), Monster Raving Loonin Party ....**700 million**

No change ever again.

PUTIN'S FAREWELL SPEECH

Hello! I'm back!

"One day, Dad, all this will be landfill"

Film Highlights

Charlie Galore! (PG)

HILARIOUS Ealing comedy about a huge consignment of cocaine which washes up on a Cornish beach.

The fun starts when local fishermen find the drug right under their noses! And before the police can stop them they have all joined the Groucho Club and decided to pursue careers in the media.

You'll laugh, you'll cry, you'll go to the toilet, you'll laugh again, you'll pitch a project to Channel 4, you'll plunge into depression!

Cast in full

Cornish Fishermen......Pete Doherty
Cornish Landlady.......Amy Winehouse
Cornish Policeman.......Brian Paddick

The Book of Ehud

1. And lo, it came to pass that the Hamasites that dwelt in the land of Gaza heeded not the warnings of Ehud.

2. And they did rain their rockets, that are called Qassam, upon the sons and daughters of Israel who dwell in the city of Ashkelon.

3. Then the children of Israel waxeth wroth and one of Ehud's council cried aloud, saying:.

4. "Verily, they that dwell in the land of Gaza must be visited with an 'shoah', which is to say 'holocaust'."

5. And Ehud immediately issueth a clarification, saying that the words of his brother had been taken out of context, like unto a fish that hath been taken from the seas and placed upon the dry land, there to perish.

6. And the word 'shoah', he continueth, really meaneth in Hebrew nothing more than "a bit of a smiting".

7. Of the type the dwellers of Gaza are well used to.

8. So that was all right then.

9. And Ehud rose up and girdeth his loins and re-smote the Hamasites even an hundredfold. And there was great wailing and gnashing of teeth.

10. And the nations cried aloud, saying, "The smiting must cease. There must be a cease-smite."

11. But Ehud answered them and said, "Get ye stuffed like unto the olive that is filled with anchovy or pimento when it is placed in the cocktails that are served on the beaches of Eilat (Three Nights for the Price of One)."

12. And all the peoples of the Middle East saith with one voice, "Thanks be to Tony Blair, whose peace mission goeth so well."

(To be continued)

Killer Storms Lash Britain

Clockwise Lane on M25 Closed For Five Minutes

That Radio Four Today programme in full

Jim Naughtie *(for it is he)*: And now for the weather with Patti O'Heater. Good morning, Patti, it looks pretty grim out there, doesn't it?

O'Heater *(for it is she)*: Yes, Jim, the Met Office has already put the whole country on red alert for the extreme weather conditions that Britain is facing today, and already some places are experiencing freak winds of up to 200mph.

Naughtie: So what you're forecasting today is gales of unprecedented force, whipping up giant waves engulfing whole communities with a possible massive loss of life. Is that right, Patti?

O'Heater: Let me put it like this – if you're thinking of going out of the house today, you should only do so wearing a lifejacket.

Naughtie: Thanks for the warning, Patti. And for the latest update on the killer storms we're going over live to Ranjit Wapshott in the little Dorset fishing village of Barkworth-on-Sea. Can you hear me over the hurricane-force winds, Ranjit?

Wapshott *(for it is he)*: No problem, Jim. So far it's pretty quiet here, but we're hearing reports on the radio that we can soon expect winds of 200mph, creating a huge tsunami which could well engulf this picturesque Dorset fishing village, leading to a certain amount of structural damage.

Naughtie: So you're saying that there's already a major disaster in the making down there in Dorset, and that we could soon be looking at a death toll running into the hundreds, if not thousands?

Wapshott: Well, we can't entirely rule that out, Jim, although right now it's a lovely sunny day down here in Dorset, with a very pleasant slight breeze.

(We hear noise of seagulls and toddlers playing on beach)

Naughtie: Pretty serious stuff, Ranjit. And what's the feeling amongst all the ordinary people of Barkworth who are in imminent danger of losing their lives?

Wapshott: Yes, Jim, earlier I spoke to a local pensioner, Mrs Mildred Prunehat.

Mrs Prunehat *(for it is she)*: I have been having a lot of trouble with my arthritis. The doctor gave me some tablets. They don't make much difference but, on a nice day like today, it can't help but make you feel better.

Naughtie: So there you have it. The terrified face of Britain as the worst storms for 300 years sweep in...

And now – Thought For The Day with the Rev Christopher Dawkins of the Church of the Seventh Day Atheists...

Dawkins: Hullo Jim, hullo Sarah. You know, when I heard the news of these terrible killer storms killing millions of innocent people, I thought that, if God existed, he must be a very unpleasant person. But fortunately he doesn't. So everything's alright, isn't it? And may I wish you all a happy non-Easter.

Naughtie: Thank you, Chris. And now back to Patti O'Heater at the Met Office, for the latest update on these killer storms which are *(cont. 94 kHz)*

"How did that make you feel when they flushed your wife down the toilet?"

Alexander

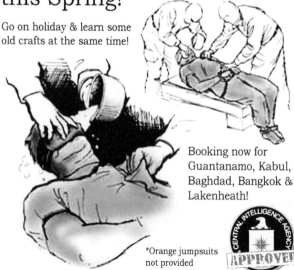

MERCENARY EXCUSES HIS PART IN 'BOTCHED COUP'

by Our Foreign Staff **Koo D'Etat**

"IT SEEMED like a good idea at the time, to depose a hated and bloodthirsty dictator and take over his oil," said the discredited mercenary Tony Blair in an exclusive interview yesterday.

Tony "Mad Poodle" Blair was recruited by a bizarre group of American lunatics, several of whom he named in a wide-ranging interview for which he was paid £500,000.

It All Went Blair-Shaped

Not speaking from the prison cell that he should be in, Blair blamed shadowy figures such as "George Dubya", a Texan alcoholic, "Donny" Rumsfeld, a born-again madman, and "Wolfie" Wolfowitz for the failed plan to invade the oil-rich country and depose its leader.

Said Blair, "The idea was beautifully simple, and we called it 'Operation Shock and Awe'. The first bit was easy. We flew in half a million troops and took over the country in a few days.

"The next bit was the part we hadn't planned, which was what to do next. That's when it all fell apart.

"I was left to take the blame, and everyone thinks it was my fault – but it wasn't."

Today, the ex-public school mercenary faces an uncertain future, not knowing who is going to give him a $2-billion-a-year job next.

Letters *to the Editor*

The American Politician and the Prostitute

SIR – I am sure many of your readers will have been as shocked as I was to read that the Governor of New York, Mr T. S. Eliot-Spritzen, was being charged over £10,000 for the services of a lady of the night. In my day, one could purchase the favours of a very presentable *poule de luxe* on Park Lane for no more than five shillings (and 10/- for the room) – in today's currency, say 75p. If proof were needed of the ravages of inflation, this is surely it. I lay the blame fairly and squarely on the failure of the now notorious sub-prime market, which had such deleterious repercussions for world finance and lonely gentlemen availing themselves of the good offices of the ancient and honourable profession of courtesans.

Sir Herbert Gusset (Client 6)
The Old Knocking Shop, Hooker-on-the-Game, Beds.

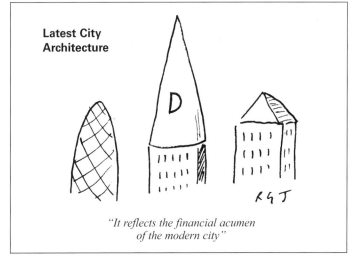

Latest City Architecture

"It reflects the financial acumen of the modern city"

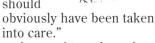
Nursery Times

.... Friday, March 21, 2008 ....

OLD WOMAN IN SHOE TO BLAME

by **Unfit Mother Goose**

A SINGLE mother living in a shoe with a large number of children sired by different fathers was accused last night of "gross neglect".

The mother, an old woman of 32, lives an alternative lifestyle in a shoe and claims "that she has so many children, she doesn't know what to do."

But social workers are claiming that the children were fed a meagre diet of "broth" and were then "whipped and sent to bed".

Said a spokes-person, "The children should obviously have been taken into care."

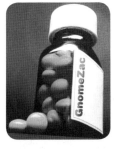

A committee of enquiry has been set up under Mrs Margaret Hodge and the shoe is to be demolished by Health and Safety officials.

On Other Pages

● Grand Young Duke of York in war gaffe: "We shouldn't have joined the Americans marching up the hill" **3** ● Four and twenty blackbirds "came out of tin", admits Old Mother Delia **4** ● Little Red Riding Ken confesses to drink problem – "My, what a large whisky you've got!" says Granny **94**

THE NEW DWORKIN BEE

Friday 21 March, 2008

'I AM DESCENDED FROM SLAVES' – Borick Obarmy's Proud Boast

by Our Man At The London Primaries **Dr Livingstone I. Presume**

BORICK OBARMY, the charismatic, front-running candidate in the battle for the most powerful office in the world, the London mayoralty, today told his cheering supporters (Sid and Doris Cameron) that he had recently traced his ancestry to humble slaves.

"So much," he said, "for people who claim that I am some kind of a stuck-up toff.

"I have now discovered, just in time for the election, that in fact my great-grandmother Mrs Ludmilla Obarmy, was a Greek slave sold by Ottoman traders to a wealthy Turkish merchant, Suleiman the Rushdie, and transported to America in the cramped cargo hold of a bendy bus."

There were emotional scenes with Obarmy weeping openly into his top hat, as he sang "Set my people free" backed by the gospel choir of the Turkish Orthodox Tabernacle Choir.

Obarmy's headline-making discovery of his slave roots was hailed as a major breakthrough in the election campaign by daytime TV celebrity Matthew D'Ancona, who said "Borick feels our pain. He will lead us to the Promised Land."

Late News
BORICK'S PHEASANT PLEDGE

Borick Obarmy today promised to replace the hated pigeons in Trafalgar Square with pheasants which could then be shot by his friends. "Who says I haven't got any sensible policies?" said the odds-on favourite in the election which has the whole of Britain talking.

LIGHTS! CAMERON! ACTION!

What's for breakfast, Daddy?

Sugary Puffs

Don't you mean Corny Fakes?

SNAP! CRACKLE! FLOP!

BLAIR TO BE GIVEN GOD JOB

by Our Man in the Clouds **St Peter O'Borne**

THE FORMER Prime Minister, Mr Tony Blair, is being tipped to take over the top job as Supreme Being, it was revealed today.

Sources close to Mr Blair said, "It is a natural progression. He is already in charge of bringing peace in the Middle East, solving global warming, ending world poverty and restoring confidence in international banking

"I, er… I mean Tony, would make an ideal God – perhaps I, I mean he, could do it on a one day a week basis between making speeches and opening supermarkets."

The leader of the opposition, Lord Satan of the Underworld, welcomed the potential appointment: "Tony Blair has already done a great job bringing war, death, famine and plague wherever he goes.

"It would be a breath of fresh air to have someone like him to work with rather than an old fashioned man with a long beard and a confrontational attitude to solving problems."

Let's Parler Anglais!

Just in!!! MOBY SUSHI

(Coming to a classroom near you)

Lesson 94: GCSE French

Teacher: Do you speak French?

Pupil: Yes.

Teacher: Vous avez passé. Next!

ST CAKES DEFENDS CHARITABLE STATUS

by Our Education Staff **Huge Grant**

Mr R.J.G. Kipling, headmaster of the prestigious, £150,000-a-term, West Midlands independent school St Cakes (motto: *'Quis paget entrat'*), today lashed out at government plans to remove charitable status from Britain's public schools.

"St Cakes," he pointed out, "has a long tradition of helping the wider community by making its facilities available to all.

"For instance," he said, "our squash courts are open to the public during the school holidays, for a token fee of only £100 an hour.

"Similarly," he went on, "local businesses can hire the school chapel for conferences, now that it has bluetooth and wi-fi facilities.

"Our Olympic-size outdoor swimming pool," he continued, "is open to anyone who wishes to use it in the months between December and February.

"And, furthermore," he explained, "we offer scholarships to deprived Russian children who have the misfortune to be born into oligarch families, and we allow them to attend St Cakes at a preferential rate of only £300,000 a term.

"Surely this is proof enough," Mr Kipling concluded, "that we are a bona fide charity, set up only to help the less privileged members of the community, such as myself and Mrs Kipling."

"This infatuation with the Mitford sisters has got to stop"

27th Beatle Dies

by Oonter Davies

THE MAN they called 'The 105th Beatle' has died. He was Ken Lurcher, 69, a softly-spoken lift-attendant at the Apple HQ from 1966 to 1967.

During these crucial years in the evolution of the most famous pop group in history, when Beatlemania was at its height, Ken played a vital role in keeping the Fab Four sane.

"It was me who kept their feet on the ground," Lurcher liked to joke, "except when I was taking them up to the 4th floor."

Oonter Gatherer

As the author of the only officially authorised biography of the Beatles, *The Beatles I Never Knew* by myself, I probably knew Ken Lurcher better than anyone else, although I never met him.

Lurcher, who had been a Lance-Corporal in the Army Education Corps, may have been the inspiration behind 'Sergeant Pepper', the mysterious band leader who became one of the iconic figures in 20th century culture.

Oonter Pants

Certainly Lurcher would have been very familiar to John and Paul, because in addition to his being the regular lift-man at their offices in Savile Row, his aunt Mildred Lurcher lived in Bainbridge Street, Toxteth, next door to Ringo Starr's mother's hairdresser, Phyllis Norman.

It was late in August 1968, that John first *(cont. p. 94)*

POLICE LOG

Neasden Central Police Station

Office hours: 9-12 Mon-Tues (except Tuesday)

0900 hrs All officers despatched to BBC to investigate serious allegation of Racial Hate Crime. A Mr Basil Brush, a celebrity fox of no fixed hole, was accused of offensive Romanyist language towards members of the Travelling community, claiming that gypsies tried to sell clothes pegs and lucky heather to the gullible and unsuspecting public. When questioned under caution, Mr Brush refused to justify his remarks and answered all questions with the unhelpful comment "Boom! Boom!" He was therefore immediately taken into custody under the Prevention of Terrorism Act and charged with Incitement to Bomb. He was, however, later given an unconditional discharge when his lawyer pointed out that foxes were a protected species under the Abolition of Hunting Act 2005.

1600 hrs Officers retire for three-hour stress management session at The Fox & Gypsy, Asda Road, Neasden.

IS SHE THE GREATEST WOMAN IN HISTORY?

HILLARY CLINTON reveals the seven moments in her life which she believes uniquely qualify her to be the next President of the United States.

4 **Hillary – first woman on the moon.** As she stepped from the lunar capsule onto the surface of the moon, Hillary famously remarked, "Vote for me."

1 **Hillary brings peace to Northern Ireland.** Hillary personally brought together the two warring factions, thus paving the way for the Good Friday Agreement which brought peace to that troubled land after 1000 years of conflict.

5 **Hillary leads civil rights movement.** Hillary inspired a whole generation of Black Americans to claim their rights with her famous speech – "I have a dream that I'm going to beat Obama in 2008."

2 **Hillary risks death to liberate Bosnia from the Serbs.** Hillary personally led US forces, under a relentless hail of sniper bullets, as they freed the besieged city of Sarajevo from the evil Serbs.

6 **Hillary's Gettysburg Address ends Civil War.** Often wrongly attributed to Abraham Lincoln, the famous speech after the battle of Gettysburg establishes her reputation as the finest orator of all time.

3 **Hillary – the secret heroine of 9/11.** Hillary personally directed the heroic efforts of New York's firefighters as they saved thousands of lives as the Twin Towers collapsed.

7 **Hillary and the Cherry Tree.** When, as a girl, Hillary was upbraided by her father for chopping down his prized cherry tree, she famously responded, "I can tell a lie – it wasn't me, it was that little boy next door, George Washington."

la Repubblica

Nation Falls For Glamorous Bruni

by Our Political Staff **Glenda Slaggliatelli**

Londra, Tuesday

THE ENTIRE country has gone Bruni-crazy as gorgeous Gordono Bruni has seduced everyone with his chic style and his surly frown *(Is this right? Ed.)*

As soon as he stepped out of Number Ten with his designer M&S grey suit and Tie-Rack tie, Bruni knocked them dead.

Il Shocko

Even those sceptics who had been determined not to like Bruni were won over by his extraordinary charisma and personal charm.

"We've never seen anything like it. I've gone weak at the knees!" said one open-mouthed admirer,

Ed Balls. "Bruni has previously been associated with some of the world's most glamorous women, including Jacqui Smith, Harriet Harman and Dawn Primarolo – but now he has become the biggest political pin-up since James Chuter-Ede." *(Who he? Ed.)*

Madame Carla Bruni-Sarkozy
An Apology

IN COMMON with all other newspapers, we may have given the impression in recent weeks that we held a low opinion of Madame Carla Sarkozy née Bruno, considering her in some way an unsuitable consort for a French Head of State.

Headlines such as "Sarko's French Tart Leaves Bitter Taste", "Carla Nudi Gets French Knickers In A Twist" and "Jagger's Ex-Shagger Marries Top Frog" may have contributed to this unfortunate misunderstanding.

We now realise that there was not a jot or scintilla of truth whatsoever in any of the above and that Madame Sarkozy is in fact a symbol of French elegance and chic, a Gallic icon comparable to Coco Chanel, Brigitte Bardot and the Eiffel Tower. She is, moreover, the new Jackie Kennedy and the new Diana, Princess of Wales all rolled into one – seductive, breathtaking, dignified, elegant... Phwooar!? Cor!?! Quelle scorcheuse!!

We would like to apologise unreservedly to the First Lady of France for any distress caused by our earlier reports.

ON OTHER PAGES: ● *Those Nude Carla Pix In Full 2-94.*

My wife is the new Diana

Tell her to wear her seatbelt

That British-French Royal State Bonkquet Menu In Full

Crudities
Frog's Leg-over on Garlic Bed
Bruni Windsor Soup
Minestosterone

– ✢ –

Filly of State with Newd Potatoes
Breast of Spring Chicken with French Has-Bean
Goose
Droules Marinières

– ✢ –

Petits Phworrs
Cheese: Old Goat's (with a Cracker)

– ✢ –

TO DRINK:
53-year-old French Randy (Cor!voisier)
Eau de Vie-agra

The Regimental Band of the Queen's Own United Emirates played a selection of hits from Mozart's "Sarkozy Fan Fruity"

Let's Parlez Franglais!
avec Kilometres Kington (en retard)

Numero 94

Le State Visit à Grande Bretagne de President et Madame Sarkozy

La Reine: Bienvenue à l'Angleterre. Êtes-vous come far?

Sarko: Oui, naturellement! Je suis President de France et voilà ma femme, le très sexy Carla Tutti-Frutti!

Le Duc d'Edinburgh: Phew! Quelle scorcheure! Un peu d'alright, n'est-ce pas! Vous voulez voir mes etchings, Madame?

Madame Sarko: Ooh-la-la! Vous êtes un one!

La Reine: Et qu'est-ce que *vous* do, Madame Sarko!

Madame Sarko: Je *do* Monsieur Sarko! Et previeusement une grande ligne des hommes, including votre own Monsieur Jagger!

La Reine: Nous ne sommes pas amusé!

"He loves the sight of his own voice"

ZIMBABWE CRISIS TALKS

I'll resign if I can keep my job

Anything you say boss

i'm very concerned about the surveillance society

i know

M.P.

WiLDur.

BROWN CALLS FOR IRAQ INQUIRY 'But Not Yet'

by Our Political Staff **Sirge Trevor Macdonald**

THE PRIME MINISTER announced today that he will have an inquiry into the Iraq War, but not while Labour MPs were still serving in the House of Commons.

"These men and women are on the front benches, risking their political lives on a daily basis," he said.

"It is not fair to them to pick over the reasons for the conflict while they are still in danger of losing their seats."

When asked how long the inquiry would have to wait, Mr Brown said, "Our brave boys and girls have a job to do and they will be there at least for another two years and possibly more."

He continued, "Morale is desperately low, as they face constant attack in the media. And when they go home to their constituencies they are not treated as heroes, but are subjected to abuse and ridicule.

"No," he concluded, "our MPs are doing their best and they deserve a lot better than some dismal inquiry suggesting they are useless."

PROTESTS OVER ZIMBABWE ELECTION IRREGULARITIES

by Our Zimbabwe Correspondent
Gerry Mander

A SPOKESMAN for Robert Mugabe's Zanu PF party has confirmed that a number of election officials have been arrested over voting irregularities.

"There appears to have been numerous examples where millions of votes cast for the opposition MDC party were counted, and not thrown in the bin or fed to the goats, which is certainly highly irregular."

In other cases ballot boxes which would once have been stuffed with votes from dead people for the Zanu PF party, and with the dead people themselves, were instead filled with actual genuine ballot papers supporting the MDC.

Said the spokesman, "This kind of activity is highly democratic and needs to be stamped out immediately."

Those Zimbabwe Election Results

Matabeleland West: F.B. Mugabe (no relation) ZANU PF, 2; P.B.W. Muzorewa, Movement For
Getting Rid Of The Tyrant Mugabe, 106,412.

(ZANU elected. No change)

Harare South: Beatama M'Bully, ZANU PF, 3; Rev Jeremiah Nkomo, Movement For Overthrowing The Hated Despot Mugabe, 164,126.

(ZANU elected. No change)

Bulawayo East: Auberon Waugh-Veteran, ZANU PF, 0 *(That's enough rigged election results. Ed.)*

VOTE OBAMA

RGJ

"Boy, you must really hate Hillary Clinton"

GLENDA SLAGG

FLEET STREET'S CHEEKIEST GIRL!? (GEDDIT?)

■ HATS OFF to Alison Pearson, my courageous colleague who's not afraid to say Princess Beatrice is a big fat lump – just like her mum!?! Good on you, Alison!?! It takes guts to point out someone else's guts (Geddit?) – and you've got plenty of them, haven't you Alison!?!! No offence fatty!?!!

■ SHAME ON you Alison Pearson, the *Daily Mail*'s so-called answer to yours truly!?! Fancy calling Princess beautiful bubbly Beatrice "fat"!?!! You're one to talk, Alison darling – I notice they don't put a picture of *you* in a bikini at the top of the column!?!! Alison Pearson!?? Alison Pear-Shaped, more like!!? No offence dearie but here's a fashion tip from Auntie Glenda – buy yourself a sarong and put it over your head!?!!

■ FOR GOD'S sake lay off Amy, Mister Pressman!?! Winehouse, I'm talkin' about, stoopid!!? Can't you see this gal's got troubles bigtime!?! With hubby in clink and being hooked on everything – especially trouble!?! – she needs some TLC, and not the media a-snappin' and a-pappin' every time she falls over in the gutter!!?!

■ AREN'TCHASICKOFHER?! Amy Winehouse, I'm talkin' about, stoopid!?! OK, so she's won every award under the sun but the only award she'd get from me is Junkhead of the Year!?! And I don't give those out too often!!?! Take a tip from Auntie Glenda, Amy – top yourself before it's too late!!?!

■ IT HURTS me to say this, but isn't it time Kate and Gerry McCann moved on?! We feel for them bigtime, but there has to come a time when we say enough is enough and try and get on with the rest of our lives. Sorry, Kate and Gerry, but sometimes someone has to say these things!?

■ IT'S EXACTLY a year since little Maddie disappeared. So what? It could be a hundred years but we should still keep looking. Hats off to Kate and Gerry for keeping their campaign alive. I for one will be wearing my yellow ribbon for *as long as it takes*!?!

Byeee!

"You seek The World of Leather? Then you must first cross The Land of Rugs, then traverse The Kingdom of Kitchens and finally journey through The Empire of Electrical Appliances!"

MEET THE CLINTSTONES – THE PREHISTORIC FIRST FAMILY

I THOUGHT HE WAS EXTINCT!

VOTE FOR BILLARY

IT'S GOING TO BE A CLOSE RACE, HONEY BUN!

YOU IDIOT! YOU BROUGHT RACE INTO IT!

YABBA DABBA DOBAMA!

VOTE HILL, DON'T GET BILL!

Don't worry honey. From now on I'm going to keep my mouth shut.

Unlike Monica!

YOU IDIOT! You've reminded everyone why NOT to vote Clinstone!

He's played the racy card!

YABBADABBA DEEPDOODOO!

You're a first-timer!

You're an old-timer!

...and I'm a two-timer!

Let's call a truce. How would you like to be Vice President?

Vice? No way! That's Bill's job!

It would be the blonde leading the bland!

OK, it's WAR again then!

YABADABA DONTGETCAUGHT CALLINGHIMBLACK!!!

I got screwed in North Carolina...

Me too once!

VOTE HILL OR...

VOTE HILLARY OR ELSE

Honey, maybe it's time for you to pull out.

Is that what Monica said?

Do you think Obama will offer me a position?

Well, I'll certainly offer his wife one!

YABADABADOOMED!

Sorry Hillary, there's only one winner!

John McCain!

It was close, but no cigar!

Unlike with Monica!

I lost and now I've got to foot the Bill!

It's all your fault!

YABADBADON'TBLAMEME!!!

New from Royal Mail

*The Royal Mail is proud to issue
a set of six commemorative stamps celebrating
GREAT BRITISH INCOMPETENCE.
Set includes: Wobbly Bridge, Wembley Stadium,
Millennium Dome, Diana Fountain,
Terminal Five and London Olympics 2012!*

**SEND £37.50 NOW TO
GREAT BRITISH INCOMPETENCE OFFER**
*(if you can find a W.H. Smith Post Office) and
we promise to lose your letter and cheque*

THAT NEW ITALIAN CABINET IN FULL

Prime Minister: Signor Silvio Berlusconi
Minister for Finance: Signor Silvio Berlusconi
Minister for Justice: Signor Silvio Berlusconi
Minister for Train Punctuality: Signor Benito Mussolini
Minister for Culture: Signora Pornella Scorchio
Minister for Women: Signora Tutsi-Frutsi Iceacreama
Minister Without Portfolio: Signor Silvio Berlusconi
Minister Without Trousers: Signor Silvio Berlusconi
(That's enough Cabinet. Ed.)

"Sorry, sire, I think I've got a cnut allergy"

SOLDIERS WIN RIGHT TO SUE WHEN KILLED

by Our Legal Staff **Joshua Rosenbeard**

IN A shock ruling today in the High Court, Mr Justice Cocklecarrot decreed that under the Human Rights Act all soldiers on active service have a "right to life".

Said Cocklecarrot, "It follows that if Soldier A, for example, should find himself in a terminal situation on, let us say, the road to Baghdad, he should be entitled to sue the Government for compensation."

The ruling has been welcomed by servicemen. Speaking from Basra airport, a typical tommy, who declined to give his name under the Data Protection Act, said, "it is good to know that we have the protection of the law. We do not join the Army to be shot at by the enemy."

On Other pages
● Lawyers welcome new ruling. Huge fees expected.

"He always felt strongly about re-using plastic bags"

WORLD FOOD SHORTAGE

'I AM TO BLAME'

admits Prescott

by Our World Food Crisis Staff
Geoffrey and Patience Wheatcrop

AS ALARM spread across the globe at the disappearance of a wide range of basic foodstuffs, Britain's former deputy prime minister John Prescott has confessed to eating all of it.

Said Prescott, "During my years in office, I was under considerable stress, which meant that I had to eat China's entire rice crop in a single morning, followed by Canada's wheat surplus in the afternoon and Italy's pasta mountain for supper."

"I had no control over my appetites," the amateur croquet-champion and luxury car enthusiast explained. "Every time there was a crisis, I had to stuff my face with the entire maize-crop of Africa. Now I see millions starving in the Third World, I feel nothing but shame."

The revelations about the cause of the current global food crisis appear in his forthcoming memoirs, Prez A Manger. They were inserted by ghost-writer Oonter Davies, at the request of the publishers, who thought the book was "very boring, particularly since he refused to write about shagging his secretary."

From The Message Boards

Members of the online community respond to the major issues of the day...

Olympic Torch Protests

"FREE TIBET" say the protesters but they seem to be young and foreigner's – do they know anything about tibet? Im study-ing this in history at college, and tibet dun a lot of real bad stuff with maggy thatcher back in the day – he ended up in jail with jefry archer and jonethen acorn. imo he shoud do his time. learn from history ppl! – *Jace_91*

I am anything but typical rent-a-mob fodder, as those who read my pamphlets will know. So why did I try to extinguish the flame? Because I am sick to death of New Labour's hypocrisy.
For ten years these so-called guardians of health and safety have lectured us on everything from smoking and drinking to the dangers of conkers. Then, with the eyes of the world upon us, we see government-picked role models like Sir Stephen and Dame Kelly waving a naked flame in front of impressionable children (and under the noses of a phalanx of burly policemen!)
Some say I am guilty of making a mountain out of a molehill (not a criminal offence – yet!) but this is how the great fire of London started. Incidentally, my costume was a giant finger (symbolising the wagging finger of the nanny state) and not the unsavoury appendage reported in the "news" media. – *Edwin*

Me agen edwin, thanx for them leaflits bruv – *Zaks_bak*

Government Backs Cadet Corps For State Schools

YES cadet's shud sort out r vilent school's ful of knife's and gun's. BUT army gun's dont work so they wud be put in un-acseptable danger? lol!!– *Darren_Coff*

Primary Schools Ban Gay Books

Good the school has band the book with the 2 gay pengins bring-ing up the baby pengin BUT wat about them paper-back's with the little pengin lo-go's – ok 4 concerting adult's but NOT 4 kid's? tipical nu labor fudge (no pun attended lol!) - *Darling_Deneyze*

St George's Day

IMPORTANT ANNOUNCEMENT: Wednesday 23rd April is SAINT GEORGE'S DAY. I know that no one will read this because the "moderator" will CENSOR it but I am writing as a matter of PRINCIPLE (remember that word Gordon Brown?) At least I will be able to read it myself on my computer. (Until the police confiscate it under New Labour's anti-English laws – I am therefore memorising it too.) – *Cry_for_Harry_Winston_Sir_Alf_and_St_George*

TERMINAL 5 BOSS DEPARTURE DELAYED

Going nowhere

BRITISH Airways last night announced an indefinite delay to the departure of Chief Executive Willie Walsh.

Said an apologetic BA spokesman, "We regret to announce that Mr Willie Walsh, who should have left weeks ago, has not taken off as everyone hoped. We have no confirmed time as yet for his flight and we are sorry for any inconvenience to passengers who are justifiably angry at this set-back."

The Plane Stops Here

It is believed that the problem with Willie Walsh is a technical one.

Said the spokesman, "He has been told to pack his bags. But he has lost them."

"The cat's finishing off your sudoku again!"

The Guardian | Friday May 2 2008

Letters and emails

Overcrowding at the British Library

As Britain's foremost historian, I wish to protest in the strongest possible terms at the recent very marked deterioration in the conditions afforded by the Reading Room of the British Library.

Serious scholars such as myself and my good friend Claire Tumbelin have hitherto been accustomed to enjoying the Library's facilities on our own, as we pursue the researches necessary to produce our highly prestigious and best-selling books, such as *Henry VIII – His Raunchy Majesty*, *Mary Queen Of Scots – The Secret Love Romps Of A Right Royal Tart* and *Charles Dickens – Was He Gay?*

Now, however, the scholarly air of erudite tranquility so vital to our academic studies has been shattered by the influx of a mass of "students" – ghastly, poor, young people who claim to be working for their "exams" and who have never written a book in their lives.

Would you believe it, I had to queue for over five minutes the other day before I could leave my fur coat and hat with the little man at the desk? When I eventually found somewhere to sit, I had to wait for ever for another little man to bring me all the books I had asked for, so that I could copy them out.

All the time I was having to endure the sight and smell of these awful young people, who clearly only come into the Library in order to meet each other and have sex.

I remain, yours unfaithfully,
Lady Amnesia Pinter
c/o Cutt & Paste,
Literary Agents, Piccadilly.

Great British Folk Legends No. 94

"And did those blue suede shoes in ancient time Walk upon England's green and pleasant land?"

BLAKE's famous poem refers to the legend that Elvis, known to his millions of followers worldwide as "the King", made a secret visit to England in 1958 while at the height of his fame.

The story goes that one of his disciples, St Thomas of Steele, invited Elvis to Britain and showed him the legendary streets of Soho.

Elvis is said to have told his apostle, "I am the jailhouse rock on which you will build your career".

Many years later, Peter Blake painted his famous picture of Elvis's Entry Into Jerusalem, still sung to this day even though no one knows whether the legend is true or not.

ANT AND DEC SCOOP NEW AWARD

by Our Showbiz Staff **Angela Ripoff**

TOP entertainment duo, Ant and Dec (Anthony Anteater and Declan McPartwork) were last night honoured with another coveted comedy award 'The Most Laughable Excuse For A TV Scam In The History Of Broadcasting'.

Presented by singer Robber Williams, the award is only given to someone who, in the judges' opinion, should be put in jail. *(Is this right? Ed.)*

Said Robber, "Ant and Dec's excuse that they knew nothing about anything was absolutely hilarious. I have never heard anything so funny in my life."

However, ITV chairman Michael Greed was furious not to win the award himself.

Critics had hailed his amusing

Ant or Dec and Dec or Ant

performance in not sacking anyone over ITV's phone-line scams. They felt that Greed deserved the prestious award and he agreed.

"My line about zero tolerance was much funnier than Ant and Dec's," said Greed. "This prize has clearly been rigged."

Inspector Knacker meanwhile announced that no further action would be taken against Messrs Ant and Dec for the fraud, on the grounds that they did not know which Geordie funster was which – and did not want to shoot the wrong one.

Wedding of the Century
How They Are Related

Cheeky Girl

Opik

Vlad the Cheeky	Sesame Street-Porter
Cheeky The Vampire Slayer	Opik Sesame
Count Dracula	Lemsip Opec
Michael Howard	Limpet Harpic
"Touch My Bram" Stoker	Legover Toothpic
Bum Stroker	Libdem Opeless
Gabriella Vampirimia	Lembit O'Booze
Lembit Ofallright	**Count Drinkula**

YES! IT'S BORING JOHNSON

by Our Political Staff **Charles Boore**

THE NEW-LOOK Conservative candidate for Mayor, Boring Johnson, has stunned voters in the run-up to the election by an extraordinary succession of non-gaffes.

"You've just got no idea what sensible statement he's going to make next," said one baffled observer. "With his tousle-free hair, tucked-in shirt and detailed views on inter-borough financial relations, he has really not set this election on fire!"

Boring has unimpressed voters with his new style of campaigning.

'He's wowed no one," said Londoner Mohammed Zbrwski-Smith, "and wherever he goes he doesn't come up with jokes, quips or outrageous views on minorities."

Bland Hair

But Boring hopes that his new strategy will pay dividends by making him even more boring than Ken Livingstone, with him thereby ending up as London Maybor *(surely 'Mayor'? Ed.)*.

In an unrousing plea, Boring now pledges that he will be "Tough on cripes! Tough on the causes of cripes!" *(That's enough Boring Johnson. Ed.)*

On Other Pages
■ My Five Boring Pledges For A More Boring London by Boring Johnson

Yes, It's All New Boring Johnson Cockney Rhyming Slang

Whistle and Flute	Sensible Suit
Apple and Pear	Tidy Hair
Trouble and Strife	Devoted to Wife
Tea Leaf	Youth Crime Chief
Frog and Toad	Heavy Workload
J Arthur Rank	Transport Think Tank
Rub-a-Dub-Dub	London's Finances Devolved But Accountable to a Central Economic Hub

(That's enough, Ed)

"Yes, most kids carry one these days"

Court Circular

Highgrove, Tuesday

His Royal Highness Marshal of the Royal Air Force Prince William (Pilot Officer Wales) will fly a training mission in a Chinook helicopter, Heir Force One, from Highgrove House, Gloucestershire to a rendezvous with His Royal Highness Field Marshal Prince Harry (Lieutenant Wales) at the Slug & Ferret public house in Upper Wheatcroft, near Aldershot, Hants. After a refuelling stop, during which Their Royal Highnesses will consume 16 pints of old English vodka, the training flight will continue to a further rendezvous with the Shortly To Be Royal Highness Ms Kate Middleton in a field near her Dad's house at Quickbucklebury, Berks.

The Royal Party may be joined at this point by the following service personnel: Toby Ricketson-Smythe, The Hon 'Fruity' Frutella-Marjoribanks, Rupert Twystleton-Twytte, Lady Bulimia Vomit and a number of other guests too drunk to stand up or indeed remember their names.

The flight will continue somewhat erratically to somewhere or other, possibly the Isle of Wight (or it might be the Isle of Mull), where they will have a bloody good piss-up involving the consumption of the following items: 10 barrels O'Grady's Genuine Cornish Cider; 300 bottles Bacardi Rum 'n' Nitroglycerine; 1600 cans of 'Beijing Bomber' Chinese lager and one packet of Osama's Pork Scratchings.

The Royal Helicopter will then be commandeered by the RAF Medical Corps to take them to the nearest A&E Department to resuscitate the survivors of "Operation Legless".

Wednesday

Their Royal Highnesses will receive Campaign Medals for Services to the Drinks Industry. *(That's enough Court Circular. Ed.)*

Hunt continues for story to replace Maddie

The Daily Express is still appealing to anyone who has seen a story that will replace Maddie. The owner of the Express, Mr Dirty Desmond, made a tearful appeal last night.

"I have lost a huge amount of money paying off the libel bill and I am desperate to find a way of getting it back."

Continuing our serialisation of Cherie Blair's sensational memoir **Helping Myself**

(Littlegordonbrown, £29.99)

Chapter 92
Bundle Of Joy

WHAT a weekend it was! Tony and I were staying in Balmoral with the dreary old Queen when I discovered to my surprise that I had a little book on the way! Imagine – at my age!

Obviously I was thrilled for myself, but how would Tony take it? He had other things on his mind, like the terrible war with Gordon Brown.

However, when I broke the news, instead of looking worried his face broke into a huge smile. "How wonderful, darling!" he said. "I've always wanted some more money."

It was such a relief to know that he was going to support me through all the sleepless nights during the nine months of hard labour it took to produce the book.

Chapter 93
A Nasty Surprise

A VISIT to the publishers confirmed my worst fears! The book is going to be four months premature! My publisher is desperately worried that Gordon might be gone by the time our baby arrives, and then it might be too late!

Wouldn't that be awful? All that effort and no money at the end of it!

Chapter 94
The Delivery

UNFORTUNATELY a lot of other people are having books at the same time as me. John Prescott and Lord Levy have both had one already!

"Never mind, darling," said Tony. "Yours will be special!"

And so it was. The book came out and a lovely £500,000 non-bouncing cheque was delivered safely through the door of Number Ten Downing Street.

Tony was overjoyed. He picked it up and held it lovingly in his hands.

"You beautiful little cheque!" he said. "I'm going to take you for a little walk down to the bank right away."

TOMORROW: How I always had the utmost respect for the melancholic, psychotic, fat Scots git Gordon Brown who ruined my husband's life. Oh yes, and how Carole Caplin made me really thin.

"And this is me at Uni. Like all of us, I had a lot more hair in those days..."

New From Gnome

THE CHERIE BLAIR
CONTRACEPTION KIT

'THE BALMORAL'
At last, family planning made easy!

Simply leave this handy device at home (in drawer or under bed) and... hey presto, bun's in the oven!

As approved by His Holiness The Pope!!

LEADER SUFFERS TERRIBLE DEFEAT

I feel your pain. I am listening. The relaunch starts here...

BLAIR ADVISES BELEAGUERED BROWN

I'd invade Iran if I were you

WEST END FLOP!

GONE WITH THE WINDBAG

SET against the backdrop of Labour's Civil War, this epic saga of jealousy and revenge tells of the doomed triangular relationship between **Scarlett O'Blara**, **Cashley Blair** and **Rhedd Brown**.

Featuring the great Southern hit songs:

Gordon Brown's Body Lies A-Mouldering In The Grave

Swannee (We're all Going Down The)

Mine Eyes Have Seen The Glory Of The Coming Of Lord Levy

Tory Tory Halleluia!

EYE RATING: Z-z-z-z-z-z-z

A Dictionary of the English Language

Dr Boris Johnson

Buffoon statesman-like figure capable of occupying the highest civic office

Cripes exclamation expressing disbelief, as in 'Cripes, I never thought I'd win'

Guppy (a) species of fish; b) frightful crook educated at Eton and one-time close friend of the lexicographer

Spectator magazine providing useful employment for hacks

hired to assemble the pages while the editor is enjoying a long lunch with his ladyfriend

Legover vulgar expression referring to pleasurable amorous diversions *(see entry above)*

Cycle lane special lane on the highway designed for the exclusive use of important political figures such as myself and my friend 'Oofy' Cameron

Petronella antique dance of the type a trusting wife might be led by an unfaithful husband

Cripes expression of disbelief used by such a husband when his amorous exploits are revealed to the world's newsmen *(see above passion)*

(That's enough dictionary. Ed.)

> *"He who is tired of being Mayor of London is ready to become Prime Minister"*
>
> The Wit and Wisdom of Dr Boris

"You'll never believe what my house isn't worth"

EXCLUSIVE TO ALL NEWSPAPERS

BURMA CYCLONE TRAGEDY

By Our Disaster Staff Phil Graves

THE BURMESE government say it's a tragedy that 60,000 of it's countrymen have died at the hands of Cyclone Nargis.

"These people should have course have died long lingering deaths in state-run concentration camps at our hands" said a furious government spokesman.

The Burmese government has meanwhile asked the international community for urgently needed weapons, following the devastation wreaked by Nargis.

"We urgently need semi-automatic weapons, land mines, stun-guns, armoured grenade launchers and intercontinental missiles to help our people recover from this terrible tragedy," said a senior Burmese general.

Those Burmese Government Plans To Deal With Cyclone Threat In Future

● Place all cyclones under indefinite house arrest.

● Err...

● That's it.

We're putting the Goon into Rangoon

"We just want to welcome you to the village and hope that you'll be very happy here"

An Open Letter To Peaches Geldof

Dear Peaches,

Like many concerned columnists, I have read about your recent antics with mounting alarm. The drinks, the drugs, the parties, the boyfriends – it is all too reminiscent of your poor late mother whom I nearly met once. I watched her too fighting a losing battle with her inner demons, taking a downward spiral to self-destruction and I remember clearly writing an open letter to her as well.

Peaches, I've seen your father on television, so I know exactly what he must be going through, as he watches helplessly an eerie replay of the past unwinding before his sad eyes.

So let me make this plea to you, Peaches, woman to woman: *please, please, please* keep on getting drunk, stoned and behaving badly, so that I and others will have something to write about.

For God's sake, don't stop before it's too late! And with any luck you will heed this message and become a role model for your siblings, so that I can write about them going off the rails as well.

Your caring friend,

Polly

© P. Filler 2008

POLICE LOG

Neasden Central Police Station

0900 hrs All officers were summoned to a staff association meeting to discuss the right to take industrial action in pursuit of our 104 percent wage claim, backdated to 1954. Elevenses and lunch were provided. Motion supporting strike was unanimously carried.

1214 hrs Emergency call from the N. Ron Hubbard Memorial Hall to say an unauthorised protest was taking place outside the premises, threatening a major breach of the peace. The entire force was deployed to the address in question, with which we were familiar, having enjoyed the hospitality of the Church's Chief Thetan, Mr Gilbert Rowbotham, only the previous evening. The Chief Thetan, moreover, had flown in from Mars especially for the occasion. We would like to record our thanks for an excellent dinner and some fine Californian wine (Premier Tom Cruise), rounded off with a very enjoyable showing of Mr Travolta's latest film, Battlefield Earth III.

On arrival at the Hubbard Tabernacle, officers discovered a mass demonstration involving a 12-year-old boy, Wayne Dimple, carrying an inflammatory banner reading "Down With Scientology". The boy, who cannot be named for legal reasons, was arrested under the Incitement To Religious Hatred Act 2004.

Whilst travelling to the hospital with the now-injured suspect, the vehicle driven by PC Morden was involved in a 100mph collision with a young female pedestrian, who suffered an immediate terminal experience.

When members of her family suggested that PC Morden might in some way have been responsible for the young person's demise, it was necessary to restrain them by 1000-volt Taser from expressing totally uncalled-for and abusive comments designed to lower the police service in the esteem of the law-abiding community. Unfortunately, two of the subdue-ees failed to recover.

NOTICE: There will be no change to our Bank Holiday service to the public, when the station will be operating as normal – i.e. it will be closed. Any members of the public in need of emergency assistance may contact our counselling service, which has been outsourced to Ganesh Call Centre Solutions in Bangalore on 0877 614 23781.

Fountain and Jamieson

WEDDING OF THE CENTURY

In collaboration with *Hellohaveyoucomefar* magazine, *Private Eye* presents a unique guide to the Royal Family of tomorrow that is taking Britain into the 21st century.

① Lady Rhiannon Starborgling, 23, second-cousin twice removed of Lord Bluewater, Keeper of the Royal Toastrack to Her Majesty the Queen.

② Reg Kwikfit, 54, step-uncle to the bride Autumn O'Beal, proprietor of the Moosejaw Exhaust Center in Edmonton, Canada.

③ Rupert Ricketson-Smythe, 24, brother of the best man Pongo Ricketson-Smythe – both were at Eton with David Cameron and Boris Johnson. Rupert had to hire his wedding suit from Schilling and Lom, Gent's Outfitters of Slough, having mislaid his own

during stag night at Slapper's night club organised by the groom's brother-in-law Lord Harry Voletrouser (see 16).

④ Mrs Mabel Leaf, 73, (half-sister of bride Autumn Leaf), formerly married to Reg Kwikfit's brother Bruce T. Leaf, a radio presenter on the popular "Good Morning, Ontario" drivetime show.

⑤ Princess Euphorbia, 19, grand-daughter of Her Majesty The Queen through her father the Duke of Gwent. Currently studying at the London School of Reflexology.

⑥ Miss Sally Middleclass, 21, currently in on-off meaningful relationship with His

Royal Highness Prince Hooray which may lead to future "supportive parenthood" role in royal family.

⑦ Gilbert Dressage, 53, fellow equestrian friend of the Princess Royal, who shared bronze medal at the Oslo Olympics in 1981 on the legendary Desert Storm.

⑧ Obadiah Omo, 32, the first Polynesian islander to join the Royal Family through his sister's marriage to the Hon. Frederick Marshmallow who, as the great-great-nephew of the late Lord Mountbatten, is 78th in line. *(That's enough Royals. Ed.)*

Order Of Service

Conducted by the Right Rev. Sandra Dross, Editor-in-Chief of Hello! Magazine

Introduction

Dross *(for it is she)*: Hello!

Congregation: ¡Hola!

Dross: Let us pay.

Bride & Groom: Thank you very much.

The Marriage

Dross: Do you, Peter Philboots, and you, Autumn Kello!, take this cheque to have and to hold, for richer and even richer, until you both shall divorce and then we'll cover that as well?

Bride & Groom: I do.

Dross: I now pronounce you £500,000 better off.

Reading

There shall then follow a reading from *"The Profit"* by Khalil Gibran.

Hymn

The congregation shall then join in the hymn *"Now bank we all our stash"* or it may be *"Love of money divine, all loves excelling"*.

The Signing Of The Contract

Here the bride and groom will sign an exclusive deal with Hello! magazine, in which they will promise to forsake all other publications and give the pictures only to their lawful partner, ie Hello!.

Dismissal

The Queen's objections will be dismissed by the groom.

Groom: Shut up, granny. We're broke.

Congregation: Yah, shut up, misery guts!!!

Procession

The laughing couple will then proceed to the bank. It may be HSBC Windsor High Street (M. Faversham, Assistant Manager) or TSB Slough (G. Popplewell, Chief Cashier).

Organ Voluntary

(followed by the Photo Involuntary)

"My Sweet Loot" by George Harrison, played by organist R.R. Ingrams.

"By anyone you know?"

HEATH

DIARY

THE RT HON
JOHN
PRESCOTT MP

It's 2005 or thereabouts and I'm sat at an official banquet in the Guildhall I think it were, next to the Queen of the Neverlands, I forget her full name, Her Royal Majesty Something-or-Other, and enjoying tucking into my starter.

"Only trouble with Prawn Cocktails," I say to her as I lick my spoon, "is that they're always too small, don't you find?"

The lady mutters something. As I'm reaching for the bread and butter, I notice there's still the heck of a lot of Prawn Cocktail left in her glass dish and she's just pecking at it. So to help her out, I say: "Tell you what, we'll swap dishes – you take mine and I'll take yours! That way we'll both be happy! Vous comprenay?"

And with that, I reach out for her Prawn Cocktail – retaining my own spoon, I don't want to catch her foreign germs – and I polish it off there and then, even the lettuce, leaving the plate nice and clean.

"Very tasty!" I say, patting my stomach in a light-hearted gesture but being royal and foreign – not that I've got anything against foreigners, mind, it's just their food I can't abide! – she's very stiff and doesn't respond.

So I turn to the gentleman on my right, the President of Venice or Venezuela or whatever, and try to break the ice. "Not finishing your Prawn Cocktail then, Pedro? Defeated you, has it?"

The guy looks back at me as though I'm talking double-dutch, so I speak louder. "DEFEATED YOU HAS IT?"

To set him at his ease, I reach over, shove my spoon in his Prawn Cocktail and help him out with it. And very tasty it is too, very tasty indeed.

"Much-o grassy-arse, mon amigo!" I say with a pleasant chuckle, very slow so's he'll understand, and grab myself another couple of bread-rolls before the waiter runs off with them.

Come my main course, the old tum is up to its tricks again making me feel I'm full when I'm not but I don't want to miss out on the meat course – I've always loved my meat – so I seek to remedise the situation. I look over the President's shoulder, very discreetly you understand, for a toilet. But there isn't one within a hundred yards, and I don't want to disruptify the banquet, but on the other hand I have no intention of going without, so while the President's talking to the person on his right and the Queen's talking to the person on her left I reach for the old napkin.

I were once Chief Steward, so there's nothing you can teach me about napkin-folding. In seconds, I've folded my napkin into the shape of a bucket, and am just adding the finishing touches to the handle and preparing to do my business when Queen Snooty of the Neverlands turns round and asks me where exactly I live blah blah blah.

No way am I going to let chit-chat get in the way of me and my meat so I pass her the napkin-bucket and say to her, very polite, "Hold this, Your Majesty, if you'd be so kind," then poke my little finger down my throat and have a right good sick-up into it, all very discreet, mmm, that's better, wipe the old mouth nice and clean then repossess my napkin-bucket and remark "You won't be needing that no more, thanks most kindly."

I stuff the napkin in my right-hand jacket pocket and carry on with my supping. The meat is beautifully tender and the potatoes just right. The soufflé is a little over-done, but the portions are reasonable and service prompt.

After dinner, we're ushered out into a great hall for liqueurs and coffee and Elizabeth Shaw mints, which I've frankly never liked, they're too small, but luckily I've taken the trouble of hiding a tin of Condensed Milk behind a curtain on the way in so I make my excuses and polish it off in the vestibule.

So we're all milling around in the hall with our coffees when Tony beckons me over saying, "John, there's someone here I want you to meet!" It's Henry Kissinger, no less. I want to give the right impression, so I stick my right hand in my jacket pocket, all suave-like, as I make my approach.

"Dr Kissinger," says Tony, "may I introduce my Deputy Prime Minister?"

"Delighted to meet you, I'm sure," I say, all sophisticated. I pull my right hand out of my jacket pocket and give his a good strong shake.

"Mein Gott!" says Kissinger. We all glance down. There's this gooey stuff, bitty and that, dripping off his hand. Tony throws me one of his looks, as if to say it's all my fault! But as I told Pauline after, you can hardly call it my fault if they don't provide accessible toilet facilities at these hoity-toity venues, it's high time something was done about it, it's always the working classes what get the blame and the chinless public school brigade who are let off scot-free, so those of us who, for reasons of pressure and stress at work, sometimes putting in sixteen, seventeen, eighteen hours a day, find it necessary to sick up our food, should be given every facility for so doing.

I attempt to make light of the goo with our distinguished guest. "Wipe it off, Henry! What do you think sleeves are for?!" I jest. But he doesn't see the funny side. Very German!

As told to CRAIG BROWN

New BBC Thatcher Play Reveals Shocking Affair

by Our Media Staff **Phil Airtime**

A NEW BBC drama about the early life of Margaret Thatcher contains the explosive revelation that the former Prime Minister had a secret romance with a famous political rival.

Hampstead Heath

In the new film, the young Margaret is shown in a passionate relationship with dashing young politician Jeremy Thorpe.

Thorpe, the leader of the Liberal Party, is depicted as a notorious ladies man who makes a beeline for the glamorous Tory sex kitten. Sizzling dialogue reveals the simmering passion between the two would-be lovebirds, including the following red-hot exchange at a fringe meeting:

Thatcher: I'm looking for a seat.

Thorpe: Aren't we all, ducky?

Thatcher: I'm happy to start at the bottom.

Thorpe: Me too, sweetie! Now, if you'll excuse me, I must talk to Edward Heath.

Heath: Hello Jeremy.

Thorpe: Hello Sailor!

Says BBC Head of Rubbish, Ben Matt: "This is an extremely well researched docudrama of the highest quality and shows Mrs Thatcher's political career in an important new light."

Said the Deputy Head of Rubbish, Matt Ben: "It is commom knowledge that Mrs Thatcher was Prime Minister of Great Britain. What is not so well known is that her lovers included Quentin Crisp, Liberace, and the young Peter Mandelson."

Radio Three

Live from the Met

Berlusconi's 'The Robber Baron and the Gypsies'

Having returned from exile to his throne in Italy, Silvio, the robber baron, finds an encampment of gypsies outside his palazzo.

The gypsies dance and sing, *"Grazie, grazie a Brussels"*, a chorus of praise to the EU for allowing them to come from their homes in faraway Romania to earn their livings as window cleaners, olive pickers and workers in the crime and sex industries.

The baron is enraged and sings the famous aria, *"Sono sono ladrone"* ("I do the robbing around here"). He incites the townsfolk, with the support of the carabinieri, to attack the gypsy camp and burn it to the ground.

As they do so, they sing the joyful closing chorus, *"Arrivederci Roma"* ("Immigrants go home").

Daily Mail

FRIDAY, JUNE 12, 2008

LAWS THAT ALLOW LIVING ABORTED FOETUSES TO BE MADE INTO HYBRID HALF-MAN-HALF-RAT MONSTERS AND INJECTED INTO GM PLANTS AND GIVEN TO CHILDLESS LESBIANS COULD CAUSE HOUSE PRICE CRASH

by Our Entire Staff

THERE was outrage yesterday, as laws that allow living aborted foetuses to be made into half-man-half-rat monsters and injected into GM plants and given to childless lesbians could possibly cause a house price crash.

It was obvious that the freaks of nature created by this insanity wouldn't need houses and would probably live in ponds, causing a huge drop in demand in the *(cont. p. 94)*

NEW HYBRID POLITICAL ANIMAL

He's part Blair, part Thatcher!

What have we done?

And he's alive!

Secret Documents Found On Train Shock

SENIOR politicians expressed dismay last night at the news that for the third time this year a train had actually been running – thus providing somewhere for senior civil servants to leave secret documents.

Said Data Minister Patsy Jacket MP: "It's an outrage and suggests a systemic failure across the whole railway network."

However, a spokesman for Railtrack called it "an isolated incident". He said: "We regret this uncharacteristic error and will do everything in our power to make sure it doesn't happen again."

(Reuters)

Bank Chiefs' Cautious Warning

THE GOVERNOR of the Bank of England, Mr Mervyn King, yesterday told the City, "We're all going to die! We're doomed. Do you hear me? Doomed."

City analysts interpreted Mr King's coded remarks as an indication that interest rates might *(cont. p. 94)*

THAT WORLD FOOD CRISIS SUMMIT IN FULL

by Our Food Staff **F.A. O'Booze**

THOUSANDS of delegates flew into Rome from all over the world to discuss what they were going to have for lunch *(Surely the growing world food shortage? Ed.)*.

Attendees were first treated to a two-hour speech by Iran's prime minister Mohammed Ahmedinajacket, who blamed the Jews for eating all the world's food, thus leaving none for anyone else.

The Iranian leader's comments were greeted by applause from the Arab delegations.

Next to speak was Zimbabwe's President Mugabe, 96, who blamed the British colonialists for eating all his country's food, thus leaving none for his people.

His speech was greeted with a standing ovation from the African delegates.

Condoleezza Rice-Shortage

Finally, the Rev. "Banksy" Moon, the mural painter and religious leader who has recently taken over as Secretary-General of the UN, proposed that €700 billion should be given to the UN to organise further conferences on this important issue.

New Modest Look For Newsnight Girls

(l-r) Kirsty Wark, Emily Maitlis, Stephanie Flanders

HOPE FADES FOR MAN TRAPPED UNDER LANDSLIDE

by Our Disaster Staff **Candida Crewe and Nan Twitch**

RESCUE TEAMS were preparing to give up any hope of rescuing the man caught beneath a huge landslide that registered 17% on the Swingometer.

Said one charity worker, "We were hoping for some sign of life but I think it is time we called it a day and admitted that Gordon is beyond any help."

● Full story with distressing pics **2-94**.

Old songs revisited

Oh Mr. Porter

What shall I do? ♪

I wanted to stay in Downing Street

But they put me out at Crewe. ♫

THAT CREWE AND NANTWICH RESULT IN FULL

Tamsin Dunbadly (Labour): 3;

Edward Tophat: 278,973;

Libby Dem 2;

Others: -5.

(Toff Gain)

HOW TO LOSE VOTES AND ALIENATE PEOPLE 12A

NEW MOVIE OUT NOW!

starring

Gordy Brown

as

Toby Young

◇◇◇◇ *"Full of hilarious gaffes"* – Daily Mail

◇◇◇◇ *"Let's all vote Conservative"*
– Crewe & Nantwich Courier

"I don't care how few of us there are left, I'm not ever NEVER going through that again"

COUNTER NUMBER 4 PLEASE

Rossen

"I believe that the drug dealers in this area are quite well organised"

DRAWING ALL FAITHS TOGETHER

Hello,

You may remember me! – I used to be vicar for a little parish called St. Albions but guess what, I'm now the vicar of a global parish – and not just for **one** faith but for **all** faiths. One way you could look at me is that I'm there for everyone whatever they believe – a bit like God!

So, now I am appealing to people of every faith around the world to come together in a common cause, under my leadership, to solve all the world's problems.

Goodness me, it's not as though there are that many of them!

I've solved some of the big ones already – Northern Ireland, for one, and the Middle East for another.

So, how about this for a big idea? Why don't all of us, be we Christians or Muslims or Jews – and hey, aren't we all the children of Abraham anyway? – why don't we all get together and kill a mosquito each and every day?

And, hey, wouldn't that end the dreadful curse of malaria, just like that! There are 9,386 million mosquitos in the world – but many more believers!

So let's get mosquito hunting – for Africa, for Asia, for the world, for the universe.

SORTED!

And remember, here at DAFT, we **do** do God!

If you want to join DAFT then visit my site on **Faithbook**!

Rev. T. Blair

Chief Executive, D.A.F.T.
(former vicar of St. Albion's)

'MAKING A BETTER TODAY TOMORROW'

"We're so glad we bought petrol instead of a house"

I Say These Immigrants Should All Be Shot

says the Daily Mail's **Phil Space**

BLIMEY, guv, they've got a nerve haven't they? Coming over here to live off handouts and steal our food.

Bloody Canada Geese, who asked them to fly in? They're bloody idle too, instead of going down Hackney Marshes with all the other geese they hang around Hyde Park doing their business all over the grass, disgusting isn't it? Little kiddies could go blind. I tell you last week I picked up this fare just off St James Park and this bloody great goose came and sat on my nice clean bonnet so I told him to f*** off home *in Polish*, it's the only language these geese understand. Do you know what I'd do? Shoot the lot of them!

I had that Conrad Black in the back of my cab once with *his* Canadian bird, Barbara Amiel, blimey I wouldn't mind goosing her, eh guv... D'you geddit?

© Daily Mail

LABOUR UNVEILS PLANS FOR 750 ECO-TOWNS

by Our Environmental Staff **Patty O'Heater**

THE WHOLE of southern England is to be turned into a series of interlocking "eco-towns", each housing 700,000 people living in a totally "green", carbon-free environment.

At a press conference yesterday at the Department of Infrastructure, Urban Living and the Quality of Life (DIULAQL) the minister Patsy Jacket explained to waiting newsmen how the eco-city of tomorrow will work:

Homes

Each home will be fitted with:
- **underfloor solar heating**
- **lighting powered by recycled compost**
- **windmill-powered trouser presses in every bedroom.**

Transport

Cars will be banned and residents will travel everywhere by one of the following options:
- **sail-powered waterbuses using a canal system**
- **hop-on, hop-off hot air balloons**
- **Star Trek-style "transporter rooms"** *(not invented yet)*

Services

To minimise carbon footprint, energy-intensive schools and hospitals will be decentralised to neighbouring towns.

Huge Brazilian-style rainforests will be planted in every garden to soak up unwanted carbon and provide natural habitat for endangered species such as the chaffinch, the white rhino, the Van Diemen's Land Seahorse and the Giant Burmese Tree Frog.

Energy

To be supplied by coal-fired nuclear power plants (when available).

"This gastric band doesn't seem to be working. We'd better try another method"

-PILBROW-

A Service Of Holy Civil Partnership

To Be Held In The Church Of St Bartholomew The Simpson

(Weddings, Funerals A Speciality)

The President *(The Rev Martin Dudley – for it is he)***:** Dearly beloved, we are gathered together here in the sight of God to join these men together in not quite matrimony because we don't want to get into any trouble, do we?

All: Cheeky!

The President: We shall now sing the opening hymn 'It's Raining Amen' by The Weather Girls.

The Reading

(There will then be a reading from the Letter of St Peter The Tatchell to the Guardian newspaper)

"It is totally sickening to think that the Church of England is still persecuting half the population of this country by refusing to marry consenting gay men and women. Surely in the 21st century such stupid Dark Age superstitions should be thrown on the scrapheap of history along with the C of E itself and all other organised homophobic religions."

All: Thanks be to God.

The Ceremony

The President: If any of you know any cause or just impediment as to why this vicar should not be joined to this other vicar in holy civil partnership, you are to declare it.

The Bishop of London: I object most strongly and I sent you several emails telling you not to do it.

The President: Get lost, Beardie – this is my church and I'll do what I like in it.

All: Yeah, get lost, you relic of the Middle Ages.

The Breaking of the Church

The President: We apologise for that quite-uncalled-for interruption. Now let's get on with making history. Do you Reverend N (or M) take this other Reverend N (or M) to be your lawfully wedded... whoops, no I never said that, er... civil partnered partner to have and to hold in whatsoever way you wish until one of you finds a new friend?

The Blessing

All: Bless!

The End of the Communion

The President: You may now kiss the Church of England goodbye.

All: Byeeeeeee!

The Dismissal

(The President will not be dismissed and will do it again as soon as he gets the chance)

A Psychiatrist Writes

Dr Raj Persaud

AS A psychiatrist, I often ask myself, "Doctor, I seem to have this compulsion to copy out other people's work and pass it off as my own. Is there anything I can do about it?"

What I tell myself is that I am suffering from the condition which we psychiatrists called *Cuttus pastus plagiarensis* (or Ripov's Syndrome, as it is sometimes known).

What happens is that the patient cannot be bothered to carry out his own research,

First Drafts

I think it was Freud who said I remember saying

Pearsall

Raj Persaud

so he downloads it from other work and sells it to publishers as original work.

This can eventually lead to unfortunate side-effects, such as getting caught out and found guilty.

Unfortunately medical science has not yet been able to find any cure for this chronic problem, and the best thing is simply to carry on as normal and to blame it all on careless sub-editors and others who are in no position to contradict you.

© *Someone Else 2008*

Han-z-z-zard

Prime Minister's Question Time

Mr Gordon Brown *(Dunleadin, Lab)*: May I, on behalf of all Members, pay tribute to the large numbers of our gallant forces who have made the supreme sacrifice in Afghanistan since I announced the large numbers yesterday?

All: Hear! Hear! Hear!

Mr Gordon Brown: And may I state unequivocally that they all died for a noble cause?

All: Hear! Hear! Hear!

Mr David Cameron *(Bullingdon, Con)*: May I wholeheartedly join the Prime Minister in paying tribute as well to our heroes who, as he says, are fighting in a noble cause?

All: Hear! Hear! Hear!

Mr Nick Cleggover *(Beds, Lib-Dem)*: May I also wholeheartedly join the Prime Minister and the Leader of the Opposition in also paying tribute to our heroes who, as they both pointed out before me, are fighting in a noble cause?

Voice from Back Benches: Er... what cause is that?

(Uproar in House. Cries of "Shame!", "Affront to democracy!", "String him up!")

Mr Speaker: I must warn the Honourable Member that such a flagrant breach of parliamentary protocol – i.e. trying to have a debate about a current issue – may result in the Member's expulsion from the House.

All: Hear! Hear! Hear!

(Members cheer and wave expenses claims before voting themselves additional allowances)

"Erik! Our new ship has arrived from Ikeaborg!"

MUGABE ROCKED BY MILIBAND ATTACK

by Our Man In Zimbabwe **Harare Mount**

A SHOCKED President Mugabe reeled yesterday under the ferocious onslaught unleashed by British Foreign Secretary David Miliband.

"I am thinking of resigning," he said, "and may give up politics altogether after Mr Miliband's criticisms."

Mr Miliband had earlier described Mr Mugabe's behaviour as "unacceptable and really not on at all".

"If Mr Mugabe continues with this sort of nonsense, we will have no option but to do absolutely nothing."

Mr Miliband called on other nations to do nothing as well.

Following this attack, the 89-year-old Zimbabwean dictator was said to be visibly shaken.

"I was expecting sanctions or maybe an invasion but not a mild public rebuke from Mr Miliband.

"I shall have to rethink my entire approach to politics and will probably give up being an evil dictator in order to become a monk."

JUDGE FREES TOP TERRORIST 'BUT HE MUST STAY IN PRISON'

by Our Courtroom Staff **Joshua Rosenbeard**

A MAN described as "the most dangerous terrorist in Britain" was today allowed to walk free, provided he stays at home under a 24-hour guard by 500 armed policemen.

Mr Al Bastardi must comply with the following conditions laid down by Mr Justice Looney:

Mr Al Bastardi

(We are not allowed to show his picture under the new privacy laws)

1. He must not make any telephone calls to his best friend Osama bin Laden.

2. He is strictly forbidden from receiving any visitors, particularly Mr bin Laden.

3. When he visits the toilet, he must not attempt to contact Mr bin Laden by shouting messages down the pan.

4. He is permitted to watch television, but must switch it off if Mr bin Laden is shown, in case he is trying to send coded signals to his former top lieutenant.

5. He is permitted to have one copy of the Daily Telegraph delivered to his door each day, but only after specially-trained police experts have scanned it for any mentions of Mr bin Laden which must then be cut out of the paper before Mr Bastardi is allowed to read it.

6. A special satnav device is to be implanted in his beard to allow the security services to keep track of all his movements, particularly if he is attempting to keep a secret rendezvous with Mr bin Laden in the local Balti curry house, the Star of Basra.

7. However, he is of course allowed to publish inflammatory material on the internet, urging his followers to rise up and wage war on all non-believers.

MUGABE TRIUMPH

The opposition were soundly beaten

To death

A Johannesburg Cabbie writes

EVERY week a well-known taxi driver is invited to comment on an issue of topical importance.

This week: **Mbeki M'chete** on the problems created for South Africa by uncontrolled immigration from neighbouring countries (i.e. Zimbabwe).

Blimey, guv, those black Zimbabweans coming over here, taking our jobs and jumping the housing queue – where's it going to end? Some of them have even got a standpipe at the end of the street. No wonder people don't like 'em! Who asked them to come over here? You know what I'd do with them? I'd string a tyre round their neck and set fire to it. It's the only language they understand. I had that Winnie Mandela in the back of the cab once. Very clever woman!

EU DEMOCRACY IN ACTION

All those in favour of ignoring the Irish vote

DARLING LISTS 'WORST CONDITIONS FOR ECONOMY SINCE 1997'

1. Gordon Brown is Prime Minister

2. Alistair Darling is Chancellor of Exchequer

3. Rest of Cabinet is equally competent

4. Er...

5. That's it.

THE DAILY TELEGRAPH   Friday, June 27, 2008

Opera On Three

Live from La Scala

Vivio Silvio

Berlusconi's much acclaimed sequel to his earlier masterpiece, *The Robbie Baron*.

As the curtain rises, a chorus of magistrates, prosecutors and police chiefs exult at the forthcoming trial of Silvio, the popular robber baron who has returned from his years in exile. "*Tutti Frutti*" they sing ("We gotta you thissa time, boss"), to the approval of the watching peasantry.

Everything looks black for Silvio, who imagines that he is finally to face justice for his myriad crimes. "*Sono finito*" ("The game is up") he sings in a poignant aria. But then he is visited by his clever English lawyer, Signor Davide Mills. "*Volare*" ("I can get you off") sings the husband of Tessa Jowell.

The opera concludes with the baron appearing before the Italian people (on his own television channel) to inform them that he has just issued a new law, declaring that all court cases involving himself are now null and void. "*Nulla e voida*" he sings, to the amazement of the assembled magistrates, prosecutors etc. With one bound he is free, and the robber baron lives to steal another day.

Letters to the Editor

The Resignation of the Rt Hon David Davis MP

SIR – Whatever the denizens of the Westminster village may say, out here in the real world there is massive support for Mr David Davis in his brave and principled stand over the so-called 42-days issue. The threat posed to our way of life by Mr Al Q'aeda and his terrorist cronies is a very real one and Mr Davis should be congratulated for insisting that they should all be locked up for a minimum of 42 days.

Maj-Gen Sir Farquharson-Gussett,
The Old Post Office,
Market Barkworth, Dorset.

SIR – I have never before had any truck with party politics, but Mr Davis's brave and principled stand will have struck a chord in the hearts of millions of loyal English men and women who are fed up with being told what kind of salad vegetables, whether bendy or no, that they can buy in their shops by the faceless bureaucrats of Brussels. At last someone has had the courage to stand up and call for a referendum on the Lisbon Treaty. Hats off to Mr Davis.

Mrs Q. Cumber,
The Old Greenhouse, Rowan-Under-Pelling, Staffs.

SIR – Am I alone in congratulating Mr David Davis on taking his brave and principled stand on whatever it is he is taking his brave and principled stand about? There are far too few politicians in this day and age who are willing to take a brave and principled stand about anything, and we should give him our unstinting support for being prepared to take a brave and principled stand on a matter of grave national concern, whatever that might be.

The Very Rev. Matilda Vaughan-Roxby,
The Old Vicarage,
Yoghurt St Ivel, Cornwall.

SIR – May I be the first to support the brave and principled stand made by Mr David Davis in defence of the unorthodox strokeplay of Sir Kevin Pietersen in the recent 42-over game against New Zealand? There is nothing new in the so-called "reverse switch". This stroke was first introduced by the legendary Indian batsman the Maharajah of Satnav, who employed it to great effect in his dazzling innings of 994 not out against the Viceroy's XI at Pisspore in 1872.

To lover of the game the stroke was always thereafter known as "Darkie's Swipe", in honour of the Prince.

Its resurrection by Mr Pietersen should be as welcome to lovers of freedom everywhere as Mr Davis's long-overdue call or the locking up of terrorist suspects for an indefinite period.

Sir Herbert Gussett,
The Old Hedgehog Farm,
Stannah St Airlift, Wilts.

SURELY, PIETERSEN'S GONE TOO FAR THIS TIME

EQUATORIAL GUINEA TRIAL

The plot was half-baked, badly conceived, and almost certain to fail from the word go. It was obviously Mark Thatcher's work

DIARY

HEATHER MILLS McCARTNEY'S A-Z OF PERSECUTED WOMEN

AUSTEN, JANE: The woman became one of the greatest novelists of all time – after I'd helped her with the spelling, mind – but even then the media wouldn't stop persecuting her, asking her like "So when are you going to get married, then?" or making snide and wicked comments that she wasn't the marrying type. It beggars belief. Even after all the books we wrote together had been filmed, they were still on at her with their made-up lies, calling her stuck-up and saying, "Why'd you wear those prim, stuck old-fashioned dresses, Jane, when you could be wearing hot pants and that?" I feel for that lady, I really do.

BOLEYN, ANN: Like me, Ann spent her whole life protecting her husband, even though she knew the whole truth about him. She never wanted to be Queen, she just wanted to do her charity work, but they forced her to wear that crown and live in all the trappings of wealth, even when they knew that's not what she wanted. And then her husband goes and chops her head off! And let me tell you that's exactly what's going to happen to me – I'll be looking in the mirror one day, minding my own business, perhaps looking after one of my charities, when someone – I'm not saying who, because I don't want our daughter to think the worse of him – will come along and chop my head off when I'm not ready! I've already lost one limb at his hands, I can't afford to lose another, it makes me so angry, it really does.

DIANA, PRINCESS OF WALES: I know what she went through, poor lass, because to be honest I was the only one with her in the car that day who managed to get out alive. I've never really got over the guilt, because it was me the paparazzi were chasing, not her, so I feel that I caused the accident. We were best friends, me and Diana – we had beds next to each other at school, then later I was her chief bridesmaid, after I'd ditched Charles to let her have a chance – so I know what I'm talking about and sorry but I'll sue anyone who says I don't.

GODIVA, LADY: She was a feisty lady just like me, so they persecuted her for it and burnt her at the stake. Okay, we both did a bit of glamour modelling, but that's not against the law. The way people go on about it, you'd think I posed stark naked, but for both of us it was very spiritual and I gave all my earnings from it to my charities, but I don't know if she did, we never talked about it.

LLEWELYN-BOWEN, LAURENCE: What are we as a nation doing to that poor woman, that's what I want to know. We're forcing her to decorate and redecorate her house every single day of the week, it's just not fair, and then we say, "Okay, now you've redecorated your own house you can redecorate someone else's for a change". It's mindless cruelty, that's what it is.

NIGHTINGALE, FLORENCE: I was a nurse in the Crimea, and believe me, it's no easy job walking around with your lamp, tending to all those brave soldiers with blood spurting out of them, hearing their last words, wrapping them up in bandages and that. So why are the media always going at poor Florence? She's just doing her bit, for God's sake, but they can't understand that, can they, so they try and make out she's only in it for the publicity. You know, I don't tell people this, but when I came back from the Crimea, I founded Great Ormond Street Hospital for Sick Kiddies, but I don't go on about it, it's a secret.

QUEEN ELIZABETH II: She never asked to be put on those stamps, she's a very private lady, but everyone jumps on the bandwagon and they gag her and they say "You're bloody well going on those stamps or else" and so they push her to the edge and they make money out of her misery. She's been waving at us for help for so long but we've ignored her but now I intend to take a stand. I'm going in there and saying to her, "Look, you've been Queen for long enough. You must be going out of your mind. It's time someone else took over. Pass me that crown, love, and we'll say no more about it."

THATCHER, MARGARET: I remember that last day in Downing Street, I gave her a great big hug and I said, "You go out there with your head held high, Margaret – and promise me you won't cry". But the paparazzi were merciless, even taking photos of her when she was trying to say her farewells. No wonder the lady burst into tears, for pity's sake. Have we as a nation no heart?

VIRGIN MARY: I'm one too, I know it's not easy. The Virgin Mary appeared to me in my grotto last week, and she said, Heather, love she said, you and me both, we've done such wonderful work down here on earth, but do they thank us for it? Do they heck as like!" Then she complained she had this sore back, and I hate to see anyone in pain so I laid my hands on her and I cured her. Now they're planning to build a shrine to me in my own back garden, where pilgrims can visit from all over the world and worship and I find that hard to come to terms with because I hate all this publicity. When I was in The Beatles, I wrote "Lady Madonna" about her, but someone who shall remain nameless stole all the credit for it as per usual but I don't want to diss him in public 'cos he's the father of my daughter, and I just want her to think well of the thieving bastard.

As told to CRAIG BROWN

POLLY FILLER

THEY say that exams are getting easier. Well they are not! Take it from me, they are hell. I've just been through Charlie's SATs and they were the toughest three months of my life. Easy? You try organising extra tuition across the curriculum for an incredibly bright seven-year-old, albeit one who is classified as Differently Gifted by the staff at St. Duncetans.

Then there's the supervision of the revision, at which boys are notoriously useless as evidenced by my partner Simon who ended up sitting there with Charlie watching Extreme Chainsaw Darts with Richard Hammond on the Sky More Extra Plus Plus Dave Channel!

SO WHO had to get Charlie through the vital stages! Yes, of course it was me, the only one responsible enough to tell our hopeless new girl Slavia to stop crying in her room, and come down and make Charlie do some Practice Papers. Honestly she barely speaks English, let alone French and Latin!? What do they teach these girls in Turkmenistan?

So the next time some know-it-all claims that exams are not bloody hard work I'm going to hit them over the head with my new Sex and the City Louis Vitton handbag on behalf of all the mums in Britain who are trying to juggle careers and families.

AND you know what, I reckon when it comes to Working Motherhood Studies – I've passed with an A*!

Now I deserve a week's holiday – if I can trust Slavia to look after Charlie and not to put the pizza in the DVD player! Stupid girl – it's hard to believe she's got a PhD in Rocket Science from Gurbanguly-Berdimuhammedow University! Exams must be getting easier!

© Polly Filler.

An **HEIR OF SORROWS** Special
by Dame Sylvie Krin, author of *Born To Be Queen, Love In The Saddle, Duchess of Hearts, You're Never Too Old*, etc

END OF THE LINE

THE STORY SO FAR: Charles and Camilla are watching television after a hard day at work in the new Highgrove organic rice paddy (formerly the croquet lawn)...

"AND here is the News At Ten"... the familiar soothing tones of Sir Trevor Barbados sounded above the drumming of the June rain against the French windows in the Edward VII TV lounge.

Charles and Camilla sat, as they did every night, in their matching zebra-skin thrones, a present from King Machete III of Bazuka (formerly British Bazukaland).

"Can't we watch something else, Chazza? This is really boring. Desperate Housewives is on the other side. Give us the remote."

"No, no, no," Charles remonstrated, slipping the control surreptitiously under the rhinocerous leather cushions. "I seem to have lost the thingy anyway. We have to keep up with what's going on in the world. It's very important. Look... you see."

Charles pointed excitedly at the 46" plasma screen, a gift from the Tetbury Audio 'n' Television Solutions Centre.

The screen filled with pictures of an enormous ocean liner, being towed slowly into the sunset, as Sir Trevor sonorously intoned.

"And today was a sad day for one of the grand old ladies of the sea, now going into retirement after decades of faithful service.

"The Queen Elizabeth II was loved by everyone all over the world as a symbol of a more graceful age.

"But now, sadly, she has been sold to President Sudoku of Amnesia, as a floating casino."

Charles felt a tear well up in his eye, as he took a comforting sip of his favourite single malt Glen Hoddle whisky ("A wee dram afore ye drop off").

Camilla jumped up with a sigh of impatience. "If you're going to get maudlin, Chazza, I'm going out for a fag," she said, reaching for her packet of Hockney's Full Strength.

"But it's pouring, darling, you'll get soaked to the skin. You'd better get Fitztightly to hold an umbrella over you."

"Good idea, Chazza! Have we still got that one from Harrods? You know, the one saying *'The Duke of Edinburgh is guilty'*. Bloody funny, don't you think?"

But Charles was no longer listening. He had once again been transfixed by the moving spectacle on the television screen, showing the last emotional journey of the majestic Royal ship.

A terrible sense of weariness came over him. "It's very sad, isn't it – and yet somehow inevitable..."

"IT'S very sad and yet somehow inevitable," said the newly-crowned King Charles III, as he watched from the balcony of Buckingham Palace the moving spectacle of his mother, Queen Elizabeth II, being towed away in a large lorry.

She was still gesticulating angrily at this undignified end to her long years of service, as the lorry moved inexorably into the far distance.

Charles waved a fond farewell to the old Queen as she went off to start her new life as a croupier in the Prince Philippine islands.

And who should be standing at his side but the silver-tongued commentator, now Lord Barbados of Bong, describing the scene to a grateful nation. "And so she slips away, this grand old lady. A little slower now, beginning to show her age, bits of rust appearing around the funnels – and to be quite honest, fit for nothing but the scrapyard.

"But, fortunately, the nation has a brand new replacement, fit and ready to serve."

"That's me," cried Charles excitedly, as the vast waiting crowd began to cheer, chanting "The Queen has gone, long live the King."

"Vivat Carolus," cried the tousle-haired new prime minister of England, Sir Boris Johnson, as he rode up the Mall on his hydrogen-powered bicycle.

Overhead screamed the Red Arrows, led by Squadron Leader Prince William.

And in the Palace forecourt, below the balcony, Col. Prince Harry ordered a 21-gin salute from the 17/21st King's Own Hooray Henrys.

The only person who seemed to be absent from this joyful scene was his wife, now the Queen Consort. And yet, wasn't that her voice that he could hear in the distance... "I couldn't find that bloody umbrella anywhere..."

"I COULDN'T find that bloody umbrella anywhere," boomed Camilla, standing over him in his chair, her sodden hair clinging to her head like seaweed to a rock. "But I went out for a fag anyway."

Charles dragged himself painfully from his reverie. "I was having this amazing dream about the mater. Apparently she had sort of retired, and I had become, you know, the Kingie-thingie."

"Dream on, Chazza," she laughed, as a rumble of thunder echoed round the distant Lymeswold hills.

To be continued...

© Dame Sylvie Krin 2008, The Ryanair Book Choice for June

POETRY CORNER

In Memoriam The Maharishi Mahesh Yogi, Spiritual Leader and friend of the Beatles

So. Farewell
Then the Maharishi –
As you were known to
Your millions of
Followers.

Except for *Private Eye*, who called you
The Veririshi
Lotsamoni
Yogi Bear.

"Everything passes."
That was your
Catchphrase.

And now
You have.

E.J. Thribb (17½)

In Memoriam Deborah Kerr, Hollywood Actress

So. Farewell
Then Deborah
Kerr –

Movie star
Famous for the
Steamy kiss
With Burt Lancaster
In *From Here
To Eternity*.

You were Here.
And now you
Are in
Eternity.

E.J. Thribb (17½)

In Memoriam Miles Kington

So. Farewell
Then
Miles Kington.

Humorist,
Jazz musician and
Inventor of
"Let's Parlez Franglais".

Comme vous
Might have
Ecrit,
Alors,
Adieu donc
Miles Kington.

E.J. Thribb
(Dix-sept and a half)

SO FAREWELL BUSH

Would you like me to invade your country, little girl?

I'll count you in... 1, 2, 1, 2, 7

Bom!

Er... it's 'Om', Mr President

Jeepers! A talking llama! Whatever next?

Bunny says we were right to invade Iraq

In Memoriam – Baked

So. Farewell
Then the word 'Baked'
As in 'Heinz Baked
Beans'.

You have been
Dropped, and from now
On it will be just
'Heinz Beans'.

As Keith says,
This is a very
Half-baked
Idea.

E.J. Thribb (57)

In Memoriam Jonathan Routh, TV Prankster

So. Farewell
Then Jonathan
Routh,

Star of *Candid
Camera*.

Yes, you were
Famous for your
Practical jokes on
Television.
Like the car that had
No engine.

Now you are
Dead.

But how can
We be sure
It is not another of
Your hoaxes?

E.J. Thribb (17½)

● E.J. Thribb has been reading from his new anthology *Lines On The Leaving* in the Rusbridger Tent at the Guardian Wye-on-Wye Literary Festival. A podcast of his interview with Mariella Frostrup is available at www.grauniadhaybores.co.uk

In Memoriam Dave Freeman: Author of *100 Things To Do Before You Die*

So. Farewell
Then Dave Freeman, 47,
Author of *100 Things To Do
Before You
Die*.

Sadly, you had only got
To Number 50
And then you
Died.

Which was not
On the
List.

E.J. Thribb (17½ things to do
before I finish this poem)

PRINCE WILLIAM SEIZES HUGE HEADLINE

by Our Royal Staff
P.R. O'Fensive

IN AN amazing coup, the heir to the throne, Prince William, grabbed an enormous headline yesterday when he was on board a naval ship that did its job.

The Prince was serving as a lieutenant on HMS Publicity in the Caribbean when the headline appeared over the horizon. 'HERO PRINCE CHARLIE' it said and it was only a matter of time before a routine drugs bust became the most important naval encounter since the Battle of Trafalgar.

Hello Magazine Sailor

Said one expert on military strategy, "It was a classic

diversionary tactic. The day before, the Prince had been under fire over his helicopter jaunts costing thousands of pounds."

"But in one brilliant move that story was sunk and the Prince captured a headline worth an estimated £40 million!!

MAYOR SCANDAL – CAMERON CLAIMS 'I WAS MISLED'

by Our Political Staff **Andrew Marrgarine**

TORY LEADER David Cameron today admitted his embarrassment after it was revealed that one of his exciting new political appointments had a chequered past.

He said, "I appointed Boris in good faith and thought he was the right man for the job. Now it turns out that he was not entirely candid about his previous controversial career."

Pick A Ninny

However, many senior figures are claiming that they warned Cameron some time ago that he was taking "a terrible risk" in appointing "a bizarre but flawed character" to such an important job.

The charges against Boris include:

● Using a mobile phone whilst cycling.
● Offending the people of Liverpool and Portsmouth.
● Serial womanising, and then lying about it.
● Associating with known criminal Darius Guppy and engaging in a conspiracy to commit GBH.
● Worst of all, editing the Spectator magazine for a number of years and employing Taki Takalotofcokupthenos, a notorious drug smuggler and racist.

Said David Cameron: "I promise to hold a full enquiry into Boris Johnson – after which he will have no option but to stay on."

IN THE COURTS

Sir Max Mosley vs the *News Of The Screws*. Before Mr Justice Cocklecarrot. Day One.

Sir Ephraim Hugefee *(for Sir Max Mosley)*: My Lord, I represent Sir Smacks... I'm terribly sorry... Sir Max Mosley, one of the most distinguished figures in the world of international motor sport. It will be our case that Sir Whacks... I mean Sir Max... was innocently taking part in a private orgy involving a number of sado-maxochistic... er... masochistic practices which were nobody's business except Sir Muck's... Sir Max's.

Justice Cocklecarrot: Would now be an appropriate time for us to see the video of the orgy?

Sir Ephraim: We will get on to that, Your Honour, in due

course, but I must first reiterate our case that the *News of the Screws* acted entirely improperly in breaching my client's human rights under European law to remove his undergarments and to receive correction at the hands of a number of young ladies dressed in uniforms who...

Cocklecarrot *(interrupting)*: I do think it would help if we could show the video now so that we can see precisely how Sir Max's privacy has been infringed by these terrible journalists.

Sir Ephraim: My Lord, showing this innocent scene of erotic roleplay would serve no function, but might prove painful for my client.

Foreman of the Jury: Then he will probably enjoy it!

Scott-Carrot: May I remind the court that this is a very serious case indeed, involving highly important matters of legal principle. So let us get on with the video. If the usher would be so kind as to pull down the blinds...

Sir Ephraim: I am indebted to Your Lordship.

(The case continues)

WHAT YOU WILL SEE

TopGreed BBC1

Jeremy Clarkson: This week we're putting our cheques to the test. First up Hammond.

(Film of Richard Hammond driving fast into wall)

Hammond: My cheque is much smaller than Jeremy's. Why can't I have a bigger one?

Clarkson: That's because you're not nearly as good as me you useless runt. *(Audience fall about laughing)* So what about May?

(Film of James May driving slowly in traffic jam)

May: I've put my cheque through its

paces and it's under-performing badly, particularly compared to Jeremy's.

Clarkson: That's because you're not nearly as good as me and you've got silly hair. *(Audience fall about laughing again)* So there you have it. My cheque is the biggest so I win as usual. 0 to a million quid in half an hour! Top that, Eco-Lesbians!!

NEXT WEEK: Jeremy drives all the way to the bank in a motorised wheelie bin full of money.

Numero 94

A dialogue on the vexed issue of protectionism versus free-trade avec Sarko et Mandy!

Sarko: Sacre bleu, Mandy, vous avez un nerve! Vous voulez putter mes farmers sur le dole, n'est ce pas?

Mandy: Ha, ha, ha, trés amusant, mon ami. Votre little joke. Nous sommes tous sur le meme side-vive Europe, vive le free trade.

Sarko: Idiot! Cochon! Rosbif! Vous etes un laughing stock.

Mandy: Vous can talk, matey, avec votre oo-la-la avec Mlle Bruni et votre platform shoes.

Sarko: Watchez votre step, matelot. Je suis le grand President de l'Europe! Et vous etes seulement un ami de le washed-up M. Blair.

Mandy: How darez vous? Maintenant je suis un ami de Gordon Brown.

Sarko: Il est even more washed-up que Blair.

Mandy: Ce n'est pas amusant ou clever.

Sarko: Comme vous!

Mandy: Guzzler de garlic!

Sarko: Ami de Dorothy!

(Continué page quatre-vingt quatorze)

© *Kilometres Kington*

(Continué page quatre-vingt quatorze)

CHURCH IN TURMOIL

Peace be with you

We're divided over whether we should have a schism or not

Peace off

"We want our money back"

SUMMER FAIR

KIDDIES FACE PAINTING £1

ROBERT THOMPSON

"It's a new show where Phil and Kirstie revisit all the people they encouraged to buy expensive properties"

REPOSSESSION REPOSSESSION

RGJ

SCHISM 2008
Six To Watch

Bishop Gene Kelly, 43, Bishop of New Dworkin, the first gay man to hold episcopal office in the history of the Church (apart from all the others). Gene's ambition is to see a lesbian as the Archbishop of Canterbury. "Then the Church will truly have entered the 21st Century," he says, "and it'll really annoy all those ghastly Africans."

Zechariah Onanugu, 78, Bishop of Rumbabwe (formerly the British Rumbabaland Protectorate). Onanugu claims that the Bible calls for the castration of all male homosexuals, and wants to see the Archbishop burnt at the stake as a heretic. "Then the Church will truly have entered the 15th Century," says Onanugu, "and it'll serve Beardie right for his suckin' up to all those awful shirtlifters."

The Right Rev. J.C. Flannel, Suffragan Bishop of Bluewater. Flannel has long been known for his outspoken insistence that there is a lot to be said for both sides. "The Church is at a crossroads," he says, "and it is up to each and every one of us to choose one road or the other."

The Right Rev. Bazza Billabong, 59, Bishop of New South Blighty, Australia. Billabong is an unrepentant traditionalist who believes that the Book of Leviticus has made it unequivocally clear that, as he puts it, "God's got no time for blokes who play leapfrog in the shower, if you know what I mean. And as for ordaining Sheilas, strewth, I'd rather take Communion from a drunken abo in Digger's Creek along with a congregation of Kangaroos. No offence."

"Bishop Judy" Garland, 51, formerly Archdeacon Milton Z. Krauthammer of the breakaway "First Church of Christ the Transvestite" in San Francisco. "Bishop Judy" is the first Anglican bishop to wear a dress (apart from all the others) and is said to have the largest collection of Shirley Bassey records in the world.

ARCHBISHOP LASHES REBELS

by Our Religious Affairs Correspondent **Clifford Longford**

AS THE Church of England faces its worst crisis in more than two millennia, the Archbishop of Canterbury, the Very Reverend Rowan Atkinson, last night launched a savage attack on all those church leaders who are planning a breakaway "Church within a Church" in protest against the liberalisation of the Church's stand towards women and homosexuals.

In a forthright message delivered to the leaders of FOCOFF, the newly formed Federation of Christian Orthodoxy For Faith, the Archbishop hit out at those conservatives who have been defying his authority in language more outspoken than anything heard from a churchman for more than 2000 years.

That Amazing Attack In Full

"You know, it really is time for a period of reflection by both sides, giving us all the opportunity to give considered and prayerful thought to ways in which we can each learn to appreciate the deeply held views of the other side in order to find that common ground which it is necessary to achieve the synthesis which can provide the basis for our moving together towards a... er... and now Hymn 94..."

"It's not really as much fun with everybody keeping all their money in the bank and not buying any property"

— PILBROW —

It's Your Line To Red Ken On LBC

Red Ken *(for it is he)*: Our next caller is Reg from Canvey Island. Hello, Reg. What's your point?

Reg: Hello, Ken. Did you see the final of the tennis? What a game! Would you say it was the best ever?

Ken: He's only been in the job for a fortnight and it's already gone pear-shaped, just like I said it would. There's only one rightful Mayor of London and that's me.

Reg: Thanks very much, Ken. It's a pleasure to talk to you.

Ken: Next caller is Doris from Dollis Hill. Hello, Doris.

Doris: Hello, Ken! This G8... I mean, what's it all about?

Ken: That's exactly what I'm saying, Doris. What has Boris ever done for London? Nothing. Londoners have only got themselves to blame. And it's only going to get worse, just like I always said it would. Next caller, please.

Caller: Hello, Ken. It's Monty from Muswell Hill.

Ken: Hello, Monty.

Monty: That Boris Johnson, I mean his referendum on the Congestion Charge has got to be good for London, Ken, hasn't it? Gotta admit it.

Ken: This weather we're having is terrible. Call this a summer? Nearly ruined the tennis. Did you see it, by the way? Must have been the best match ever *(cont. 94 kHz)*

BORIS/LILY ALLEN CRIME SUMMIT

Is that a knife in your pocket or are you just pleased to see me?

Why I still love Glasto

by Max Hastings

SAY what you like and you probably will – I still say 'Glasto Rocks'!

All the world and his wife have been piling in this year to say that the world's greatest rock festival isn't as good as it was in the days when I first started not going there back in the Fifties *(Subs please check decade. M.H.)*.

Well, I've got news for the knockers and the moaners – I didn't go this year and it's still as good as it ever was.

If there's one thing we British do well it's outdoor music in the summer.

The sight of all those attractive young people happily sitting on the grass in their black ties and evening gowns, sipping an agreeable class of Krug to accompany the plates of smoked salmon, is unforgettable.

And let's not forget the music. Where else but Glyndesbury could you hear such world-beating artists as Neil Diamond and the rapper Jay Zee singing

the greatest arias from Wolfgang Amadeus Puccini, whilst you muse happily on the enormous cheque that will shortly be arriving from the editor of the Daily Mail, or whichever newspaper it is that has asked me to write this rubbish.

©*Hitlertrash Productions. 2008*

Media's golden couple to split

YES! The world of celebrity will never be the same again after its most glitzy couple tragically announced that they were separating!

Shocked fans wept openly in the street as the news broke and share prices tumbled overnight.

One thinks of Bogart and Bacall! Burton and Taylor! Ken and Em. But none of them had the sheer undiluted glamour of Adrian Chiles and Jane Garvey! *(Is this right? Ed.)*

♥ *HE is the nation's favourite broadcaster, the star of Match of the Day 2, The Apprentice: You're Fired and that programme that's a bit like Nationwide.*

by Our Showbiz Staff **Dee List**

♥ *SHE is the golden-voiced part-time presenter of Radio Four's Woman's Hour and the former doyenne of Radio Five Live's Traffic update.*

Together they were 'Media Magic' and theirs was billed as the 'Love Match Made in Broadcasting Heaven'.

But it could never last. The incredible pressures of their meteoric careers meant that their relationship would inevitably buckle under the enormous strain of their stellar careers and *(That's enough over-written rubbish. Ed)*

HOW GREEN WAS MY RALLY...

A special summer short story by Dame Sylvie Krin, author of
Heir of Sorrows, Duchess of Hearts, You're Never Too Old

THE STORY SO FAR: Charles has decided to convert his beloved sports car to run on eco-friendly biofuel...

THERE it stood gleaming in the July rain outside the pagoda-shaped triple garage at Highgrove. And what an immaculate automobile it was, the Aston Martin Jarvis DD66, manufactured by British craftsmen in the legendary workshop of Huntley & Palmer in Solihull.

Charles looked at the car with unalloyed pride and affection and turned to his wife Camilla to explain the emotion that he felt rising in his tweed-suited breast.

"You see, it's a sort of metaphor thingie for everything I sort of stand for. It looks traditional and old-fashioned and it has all those values, but inside it's modern and green and ecological and cutting edge, d'you see?"

"That's wonderful, darling," said Camilla distractedly, as she climbed into the passenger seat to begin the long drive to their new hideaway holiday cottage in the Welsh village of Llegovery. "What exactly did you say it runs on?"

Charles laughed as he put on his seatbelt and adjusted the mirror.

"That's the best bit about it, old thing. It runs on alcohol."

"Like your granny, eh Chazza?"

Charles frowned. "No, no. I don't think that's very fair or very funny, actually."

Camilla tried to look more serious as Charles continued, "The whole point is that the car runs on wine – recycled surplus British wine. And it's incredibly kind to the environment. We'll get the whole way to Wales, leaving almost no carbon footprint and it'll cost us less than ten pence!"

Charles turned the key in the ignition and smiled.

"It's the only way!"

IT'S the only way," said a furious Charles, as an hour later they had only reached the end of the Highgrove Drive.

"Well, I think we should give up and go in a proper bloody car," announced Camilla, as she opened the door and prepared to abandon her husband and his treasured green vehicle.

"But we've done pretty well," said Charles.

"No, we haven't," Camilla shouted over her shoulder, as she stormed back towards the house. "We've got 200 yards and that's only because Fitztightly was pushing us."

She pointed at the exhausted, red-faced equerry collapsed at the rear of the vehicle and disappeared.

What had Charles said earlier? Something about it being a sort of metaphor thingie? "How true was that?" he wondered, as the grey clouds gathered overhead. "How very true?"

"Wow! You've got emphysema! That's so cool!"

SINGLETON'S SHOCK REVELATIONS

Here's one I laid earlier

It's *very* Blue Peter

MODERN NURSERY RHYMES

Orgy Porgie, pudding and pie,
Spanked the girls and made them cry.
When they gave the game away,
Orgy Porgie cried foul play.

NEW PRIVACY THREAT FROM GOOGLE

by Our I.T. Staff **Janet Street-View**

THE INTERNET giant Google was plunged into fresh controversy yesterday following the announcement of its new service, "Google Toilet".

This allows users to go online and download images of their neighbours on the toilet.

Protesters say that "Google Toilet" represents an invasion of privacy and have tried to prevent the millions of Google cameras now coming up out of lavatory bowls to film unsuspecting members of the public.

But Google were unrepentant. "This is a simple service that we are providing for our users – we are expanding the boundaries of knowledge and satisfying a genuine demand for online toilet-based images," said a spokesman.

"There is no question of privacy infringement," he continued, "because, thanks to us, you don't have any any more."

Google Toilet is available at www.poogle/having a slash/now-wwwashyourhandsplease.con.

MP 'DID NOT CHEAT ON EXPENSES'

by Our Political Staff **Matthew Fraud**

A STORM erupted at Westminster yesterday when it was revealed that a backbench MP had never fiddled his expenses.

MPs of all parties expressed disbelief and dismay when they learned of the extent of their colleague's failure to use public money to feather his own nest.

What The MP Didn't Do — The Catalogue Of Shame

1. He did NOT get the taxpayer to buy a second home and then charge them again for renting it out to himself.

2. He did NOT employ his wife, children or any other relatives as secretaries, "research assistants" or "policy advisers".

3. He did NOT charge the taxpayer for the services of a full-time "nanny" to look after his pet dogs, Heffer and Littlejohn, whilst pretending to be his constituency secretary.

4. He did NOT get the taxpayer to pay £25,000 for taxis to take his wife on shopping trips to the local Tesco on the pretence that the expenditure was essential for entertaining visiting heads of state, e.g. President Bush, President Nelson Mandela, President Alex Salmond of the Scottish Republic.

5. His wife did not purchase the following items, viz. ● *1 tin 'Old Gorbals' Shortbread* ● *1 case 'Old Macca's Lucky Heather Mills Single Malt Whisky' ('a wee dram afore ye gang tae court')* ● *1 Vegetarian Haggis (made in Thailand)* ● *1 six-pack of 2-litre bottles 'Dounreay Nuclear Spring Water'.*

When he was exposed as being the only MP who had not fiddled his expenses, the MP offered the House his profound apologies and offered to stand down for having brought the House into disrepute.

Han-z-z-zard

Prime Minister's Question Time

Mr David Cameron *(Bullingdon, Con)*: In the light of the Prime Minister's latest U-turn on fuel tax, as well as all his other recent U-turns, would he not agree *(pause for effect)* that he is totally **U**-seless?

(Tories erupt in hysterical laughter at extraordinary example of parliamentary wit)

Mr Gordon Brown *(Dunblairin, Lab)*: As usual, the Leader of the Opposition is completely overlooking the fact that the economic record of this government over the last ten years has shown a *(cont. 94 hours)*

The Speaker, Mick McGorbals *(for it is he)*: Hear! Hear! After that fascinating lecture from the Prime Minister which has certainly put the Tories in their place, may we turn to the much more important matter of our allowances as honourable Members of this House; and the disgraceful behaviour of the media in finding out just how much we have all been fleecing the taxpayers.

(Cries from all parts of the House of "Hear, Hear", "Sue", "Bring in Carter-Ruck", "String up the journalists".

The House then emptied as Members dispersed by taxi to John Lewis to buy vital kitchen equipment and plasma screen TVs for their second homes.)

'Britain's Kids Are Too Scared To Go Out On Streets' MALCOLM MUGGER
Daily Mail reporter

MEMBERS of Parliament were today given evidence that children in Britain today are "too frightened" to go outside their own front door in case they meet Cherie Blair.

One mother of six, Shellina Suit, told the Select Committee how her eight-year-old son Engelbert had gone out to stab his friends, but had run back into the house screaming because he had seen the former prime minister's wife.

"He was totally traumatised," she said, "and he has needed round-the-clock therapy ever since. We are suing the Council."

Mrs Cherie Scare

Another witness, Professor Horace Reebok, from the

Department of Media Studies at the Adidas University (formerly Cambridge) told the MPs, "Even though today's young people are familiar with shocking and disturbing images from their computer games, nothing could prepare them for the horror of seeing *(cont. p. 94)*

"Dave has kindly come in to warn you about the dangers of tombstoning"

SURGEONS TO GET 'NO-KILL FEE'

by Our Political Staff **Phil Coffin**

IN A bold new initiative, NHS surgeons will be given a special bonus if their patients survive their operation.

There will be a further bonus should the patient fail to contract one of the choice of superbugs now available to all hospital patients.

A Doctor Writes

MORE and more doctors are experiencing the benefits of an annual injection of money, or *Bonus porschus 911* to give it the full medical name. What happens is that the doctor may be feeling tired, depressed and out of sorts with an unhealthy bank balance. This is quickly remedied by a simple painless shot of cash into the wallet, following which the doctor will experience a sense of wellbeing and an agreeable holiday in the Algarve.
© A Doctor.

It's a sad day when a member of the Mosley family has to pay people to beat him up

IN THE COURTS

Sir Max Mosley vs the *News Of The World*. Before Mr Justice Cocklecarrot. Day 94.

(After closing speeches for both sides, the Judge gave his summing-up)

Mr Justice E.D. Cocklecarrot: I have heard the submissions from learned counsel in this vexed case involving Sir Whacks Mosley and the notorious Sunday newspaper, the *News of the Screws*.

Sir Ephraim Hugeprice has argued very plausibly that his client Sir Spanks is entitled to full privacy in pursuit of his sexual appetites, however bizarre or unusual these might appear to the unworldly onlooker. Sir Hartley Redtop, on the other hand, representing the gutter press, has put in a feeble and highly unconvincing argument on behalf of his client, claiming that it was somehow in the public interest to read about what a private individual, in this case Sir Blue Max, may or may not have done with various scantily clad young ladies brandishing whips.

This is a highly complex case involving very important issues of law, which is why I shall need more time to look again at the evidence – particularly the video which we all found so helpful last week.

I shall therefore be taking it home to give it careful study over the next week or so, after which I shall deliver my verdict in favour of Sir Muesli.

PLEASE WAIT HERE TO BE SEATED

APPLETON

More and more people these days are discovering the joys of sado-masochistic erotic practices in the privacy of their own home

Organise your own S & M orgy this summer!

Once regarded as perverse and unnatural, S & M has now become a mainstream leisure pursuit, as respectably English as croquet or fondue.

What you need to stage your own fun-filled orgy

1. Selection of whips obtainable from any reputable high street whip store, such as Whips R Us, World of Whips and Mr Whippy.

2. Selection of prison camp uniforms. We recommend Tesco's Own-brand German Officer Outfit (£27.99).

3. Genuine Military Police-Surplus handcuffs are essential (cheaper brands

"All those in favour of Max Mosley staying on..."

— Geoff Thompson

are too easy to escape from). Available on e-Bay from £105 upwards.

4. A fully-qualified 'dominatrix' is crucial to any successful S & M evening – do shop around. We recommend Rent-a-Dom of Filth Street, Soho, or the high street chain Thrashers if you want a budget version. Make sure your dominatrix is a certified member of the British Dominatrix Association, and complies with all the relevant health and safety legislation.

5. First-aid box and fully equipped operating theatre are essential. S & M can cause serious injury or even death, so make sure you have full medical back-up!

Have a really unpleasant, painful evening!

It certainly makes a change from having a barbecue on your patio or watching *EastEnders*!

Amazing Royal Treasure Hoard Goes On Sale

Those Incredible Items From The Estate Of The Late Royal Steward, William "Backstairs Billy" Tallon In Full

1. Betting slip, as used by HRH the Queen Mother, denoting a £5 wager on Fruity Boy in the 3.30pm Dubonnet Chase at Uttoxeter.

2. One signed, folded letter from HRH The Queen Mother formally requesting Mr Tallon to purchase a large bottle of Beefeaters Gin from Messrs Threshers and Co in Buckingham Palace Road "to put on one's cornflakes".

3. Souvenir Royal Ashtray, slightly cracked, bearing the legend "On the Engagement of HRH Princess Margaret to Anthony Armstrong Jones".

4. One photograph of the back of the head of a senior member of the Royal Family (possibly the Duke of Kent or possibly the Duke of Gloucester or possibly neither) taken during a picnic in the grounds of Clarence House.

5. An exquisite miniature portrait of Her Majesty

The Queen in profile from 2001, labelled "First Class 27p".

6. A wastepaper basket containing the remaining items of this amazing Royal treasure trove.

The entire collection is expected to be sold for an estimated 94p.

I'm keeping a lot of things in my closet

We know, dear

JACQUI SMITH LAUNCHES 42-POINT PLAN TO SLASH KNIFE CRIME

That plan in full

1 Leaflet to be sent to every household showing picture of knife.

2 All schools to introduce knife awareness courses, starting at age 5, leading to Diploma in Anti-Knife Studies as part of Key Stage 7 (age 11-12).

3 Knife manufacturers must display written warning on all knives, 'Knives Can Kill'.

4 Government to appoint 'Knife Czar' to co-ordinate and drive forward all aspects of anti-knife policy.

5 Any teenagers found in possession of a knife to be taken to a knife shop to see for themselves how sharp they are.

6 Nationwide poster and cinema campaign, costing £50 million, and featuring role-model David Beckham, centred on the slogan 'Give up knife crime – let's have a stab at it".

7 New punative 50p knife tax to be imposed on all knives above 2mm long – and, lest it be thought discriminatory, on forks and spoons as well.

8 A week-long 'knife amnesty' whereby any teenager who voluntarily hands in a knife at the designated local 'Knife Amnesty Point' will be rewarded with a 'rock' of crack cocaine.

9 ...er...

10 ...more parental involvement...

11 ...that's it.

"Can Johnny come out to another funeral?"

Then and Now

1918   2008

Fallen soldier   **"Fallen soldier"**

Exclusive to all newspapers

STATE FUNERAL FOR GORDON BROWN

by Our Court Staff **Damien Hearse** and **Iain Duncan-Coffin**

SECRET plans have been drawn up, we can reveal, for an elaborate State funeral for the former Prime Minister Gordon Brown.

In recent days there have been extensive consultations at the highest level, involving the Queen, the Archbishop of Canterbury and the Lord Mayor of London, to approve arrangements for Mr Brown's funeral as soon as possible.

Said a Downing Street spokesman, "We know nothing about this."

However, as the news spread, old-age pensioners and toddlers alike joined Labour MPs in hailing the scheme as an appropriate tribute to Britain's most hopeless statesman of all time.

What you will see

● Brown will lie in state for two hours in the Kirkcaldy funeral parlour of McDeath & Co.

● Members of the public (Sid and Doris McBonkers) will file past shaking their fists and shouting, "Gie us back our 10p, ye thievin' bastard!"

● The coffin will then be taken to Dundee Crematorium by mini-

cab, for a short service of thanksgiving (Speaker The Rev. T. Blair, former Vicar of St Albion's).

● Mr Brown's ashes will then be ceremonially scattered on a nearby windfarm while a lone piper (A. Campbell) plays a traditional Highland lament 'The Grey Gordons'.

● A modest collation of cold meats will be served to any mourners (see above) at the Ramada Thistle Hotel, Fife (£27.50 per head, payable at door – no credit cards).

● Parts of the ceremony will be broadcast on Grampian TV's 'News Extra' at 11.45pm.

Last night Lady Thatcher was "unavailable for comment" but said, "It's far too early to be talking about Mr Cameron in this way."

NEW SATS ROW OVER MARKING DISCREPANCY

by Our Education Staff **Phil BothsidesofthePaper**

> Pleze do not sak me Gordon becoz i did nuffink wrong, honest innit? It was all the fort of the curricu curucu correc those bastards wot are to blame you know, for hirin them yanks who cant speak English and that yeh? So pleaze can I stay on I am your only frend

THE education system received another blow yesterday with the publication of a test paper which received a pass mark of 110% when experts agreed that it should have failed.

The candidate, the 14-year-old Ed Balls (who cannot be named for legal reasons) answered the question 'Should I keep my job?' and wrote as follows:

"Pleze do not sak me Gordon becoz i did nuffink wrong, honest innit? It woz all the forlt of the curricu... currucu... correc... those bastards wot are to blame you know, for hirin them yanks who cant speak English and that yeh? So pleze can I stay on I am yore only frend."

The examiner, Mr G Brown, gave the candidate top marks for 'grovelling, buckpassing and toadying'. He called the essay 'a delightful piece of creative writing worthy of the Booker Prize for fiction'.

Educationalists however expressed concern about the spelling. One said, "This could spell the end for Mr Balls."

● Full story page 10.

THIS WEEK'S POLL: Which '70s prog rock band does Gordon Brown remind you of?

- KING CRIMSON 12%
- URIAH HEEP 30%
- YES 28%
- EMERSON, LAKE & PALMER 28%
- VAN DER GRAAF GENERATOR

NICK DOWNES

EXCLUSIVE TO ALL PAPERS

MEMBER OF THE ROLLING STONES LEAVES WIFE FOR TWENTY-YEAR-OLD WAITRESS

On Other Pages

✴ Bears defecate during extensive tour of woods.

✴ Pope cuts album about being a Catholic.

TOP JUDGE BACKS SHARIA LAW

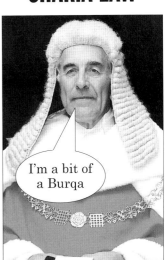

I'm a bit of a Burqa

A MESSAGE TO THE PEOPLE OF BRITAIN

FROM THE LEADER OF THE BRITISH UNION OF MASOCHISTS

Sir Max Mosley writes:

People of Britain. Today I have won a great victory for your freedoms. Thanks to me you will now all be free to exercise your inalienable right to be whipped in the privacy of your home by highly-trained prostitutes speaking in German.

But this is only the beginning.

Together we shall sweep away the reactionary forces of the prurient gutter-press, to create a pure, healthy, shame-free nation of spankers and spankees.

What could be a more glorious vision of the future of our island nation?

Join with me as I sue every paper in the land and we all sing together that rousing British anthem "Britains ever, ever, ever shall be slaves."

HEIL HITME!

(Signed)

Sir Max Mosley

Leader of the BUM (The Black Leathers)

WEEPING CAPTAIN DOESN'T QUIT

THE world of politics was not rocked to its foundation today when skipper Gordon Vaughan did not stand down after failing in another Test.

A non-tearful captain told reporters: "This is not the saddest day of my life. You know when it is time to go and it is definitely not now.

The selectors, however, have a number of names in mind who could do the job equally badly if not worse.

They include Alan "Johnners" Johnson, spinner Dave Miliband, veteran Jack Straw and Rachel Heyhoe-Harman, the England Ladies Captain.

Late Score

Labour	37 all out
Tories	381 without loss

Heath Sledger

SODOM AND GOMORRAH FURIOUS OVER 'PRIVACY INVASION'

by Our Old Testament Staff **Max Moses**

THE residents of Sodom and Gomorrah were last night threatening to sue the Bible over revelations about their sexual lives. The Bible claimed that the people of Sodom and Gomorrah had indulged in acts of wild depravity and orgies of unnatural and obscene carnality.

The people, however, have furiously condemned the Bible, claiming that whatever they get up to in private is their own affair and is of no public interest.

Said a spokesman, "Nowadays this sort of thing is perfectly acceptable and it really is no business of the Bible's prurient muckrakers to suggest that in some way we deserve to be consumed by fire."

Methuselah is 694.

WAR CRIMINAL DISCOVERED POSING AS 'FAITH HEALER'

by **Lunchtime O'Bosnia**

ONE of the world's most wanted war criminals, Tony Blair, has been tracked down in a leafy West London square, where he has been runing an obscure 'New Age' organisation known as DAFT (Drawing All Faiths Together).

Few of the residents of the fashionable square were aware that the man living at number 29 – whom they knew as 'that DAFT bloke at number 29' – was second only to his fellow war criminal, the Rev. Dubya Bush, on the world's most wanted list.

Between them the two men were responsible for the deaths of tens of thousands of innocent civilians between the years 2003 and the present day.

Blair Route

One of Mr Blair's neighbours, Lebanese restaurateur, Mr Ahmed Falafel, said last night, "He seemed a very nice gentleman. He and his wife used to come into my restaurant at lunchtime and ask for a free meal."

"I had no idea they had been mixed up in anything nasty like the Iraq war."

Mr Blair's wife Cherie was also known locally for her interest in New Age rituals, particularly the healing power of money.

The Blairs believed that if you had a huge pile of money in the bank, it made you feel 'much better'.

But now it is time for the supposed holy man to face the world's justice by being given even more money (*surely 'being dragged in front of those judges in the Hague'? Ed.*)

Boden. Summer Range

Dave, star sign *Tauries, The Bullingdon*. **Hates**: Flip flops. **Loves**: Ant and Dec shoes

Dave is wearing a safe pair of shorts with solid traditional seat and deep pockets. There are no flies, not on Dave. His outfit is topped with a matching blue lightweight polo shirt with Eton collar. Made from 100% organic Willet and designed exclusively for us by Osborne & George, it's perfect for playing frisbee and having your picture taken by the national press. Best accompanied by Hoodie *(not shown)* from the trendy 'Goveboy' Range *(not shown)*.

Accessories

Fruity wife comes at no additional cost and looks stylish, cool and electable *(surely 'delectable')*

Gone for a BURTON

ALL NEW

SUMMER RANGE

- Brown trousers with a tight belt
- Hair shirt
- Straight jacket
- Shoes you don't want to be in.

Comes with sensible wife and *(That's enough catalogue. Ed)*

ME AND MY SPOON

THIS WEEK

JEREMY CLARKSON

May I ask you if you've got a favourite spoon?

Let's face it. All British spoons are crap. I've got one here. For a start, it looks cheap. And it is cheap. And it'll fall to bits before you know where you are. Useless. Absolutely useless.

So what would you have as a quality spoon?

I know it's pricey at £180,000, but the new Bismarck soup spoon has got quality written all over it. Every bit is handcrafted by German spoon engineers and, believe you me, those boys may be Germans, but they know a thing or two about soup spoons. I suppose I am getting paid for this...

But couldn't they be dangerous in the wrong hands of an inexperienced soup eater?

Are you a lesbian or something? Or do you work for the Health and Safety brigade? If you're trying to catch me out, you've got the wrong man, sweetheart.

Are you always on the lookout for a new spoon or do you feel you've got enough already?

With computer technology, spoonmakers can do incredible things these days. It won't be long before you'll have a spoon that can stir a cup of tea in 0.2 seconds. It's just a matter of time.

Has anything amusing ever happened to you in connection with a spoon?

Can I have the money now? Preferably in cash.

NEXT WEEK: *Amy Winehouse – Me and My Wine House.*

HE CHECKED HIS FIGURES AGAIN... THERE WAS NO MISTAKE. HE WAS LOWER MIDDLE CLASS

KEY

POLLY FILLER'S ESSENTIAL GUIDE TO WHAT TO DO WITH THE KIDS OVER SUMMER

IT'S that ghastly time of year again. Eight weeks of Holiday Hell stretching into the distance with nothing to relieve the misery. How can you stop yourself from going stark staring bonkers?

Well now help is at hand. Here's Polly's tried-and-tested survival tips for what to do with the little monsters.

1. Dump the children with your parents and head for the Med – sorted! It's good for them to bond with their grandparents even if they are not as well as they used to be!?! Buck up Mum!!

2. Dump the children on the nanny and reach for the beach! Honestly – you are doing yourself a favour. She gets to see the heartwarming new movie 'WALL-E' 25 times as well as learning new skills (like industrial-scale ironing and cleaning out the hamster cage) – she even gets to improve her English vocabulary, including useful phrases like "Where do I buy wallpaper paste, your mother has told me to redecorate the nursery?"

3. Dump the children with your friends-with-the-only child! They are off to Portugal anyway and they'll be only too grateful for some company for their spoilt, annoying brat! No offence Zak and Sabrina but *even you* think Che is a nightmare!!

4. Dump the children in the Pied Piper Children's Hotel near Newbury and fly to Dubai!! Kids *love* it at Pied Pipers – whatever they say!!

5. Dump the children in summer camp. There are hundreds of camps all over England offering a great range of activities – for parents!! Like diving in the Maldives and shopping in New York whilst the kids have an old-fashioned British outdoor holiday and make new friends with some midges.

6. Look after the children yourself – only joking! Happy Holidays!

© P. Filler 2008.

Life stEYEle

EDINBURGH FESTIVAL

Six Must-Sees

The All-Male National Ballet of Uzbekistan perform Tchaikovsky's Nutcracker Suite to balalaika and song accompaniment
Venue 46725. McHackey's Temperance Hall. Seats 27

An Evening with Betty Kellogg Making a welcome return to Edinburgh, black, gay US icon Betty Kellogg tackles hot issues from child obesity to what duvet to buy.
Venue 67923. Lunchtime at Mooney's Vegan Rendezvous, 11-12pm.

Hurricane
New play by award-winning Walter Schott based on the real life drama of BBC weatherman Michael Fish facing the biggest crisis of his life – his failure to warn Britain of the 1987 hurricane. Starring former *Likely Lad* Rodney Bewes as Fish.
Venue 84861. James Robertson Justice Memorial Theatre, Princes Street, Mon-Fri.

Bewes as Fish

Work in Progress
Daring theatrical experiment created by Quebec-based Theatre du Monde. No actors. No script. The audience must fill up the six hours themselves.
Venue 89437. The Old Railway Shed, Waverley Station (That's enough Fringe, Ed.)

Royal Meetings

"We're aiming to increase our diversity quotient"

"Enjoy yourselves, but remember... drink responsibly"

MILIBAND'S SHOCK CHALLENGE TO BROWN

by Our Entire Political Staff **Sir Peter O'Bore**

THE WORLD of Westminster was rocked to its foundations last night by an astonishing and naked bid for power by Foreign Secretary David Miliband.

Making no pretence of his desire to replace Gordon Brown as soon as possible, Miliband carefully avoided mentioning the Prime Minister by name as he called for renewal and modernisation "right at the top of the Labour party".

Miliband Of Brothers

Miliband chose the traditional assassin's weapon of a boring piece in the *Guardian* to put the boot in to his leader.

In a blatant call for his colleagues to oust Brown by the end of the week, Miliband tells MPs, "Have a nice break, enjoy your holiday, forget about boring old politics, get a life."

This was widely interpreted as a savage assault on everything Mr Brown has stood for in his year in Number 10.

Although Mr Miliband was careful not to push his own claims to succeed to the leadership too obviously, his repeated use of the phrase "it is time for a modern Labour Party in a modern Britain" was widely seen as the opening salvo in the battle for the soul of the Labour Party that will soon be engulfing Britain this autumn.

MILIBAND MAKES AN ANNOUNCEMENT

Everyone can see I'm not running

BROWN MEETS OSAMA
(surely Obama? Ed)

EMBATTLED Prime Minister Gordon Brown was accused today of trying to boost his sagging image by posing for pictures with popular terrorist Osama Bin Laden.

"Osama Bin Laden has the sort of approval ratings and charisma that Brown can only dream of," said one swarthy man with a dynamite-themed belt.

"But seeing them together in Downing Street merely highlighted how unpopular Gordon Brown is."

KNACKER DEFENDS 'GIVING OUT CONTRACT' TO BEST FRIEND

By Our Serious Crime Staff **Baroness Scotland-Yard**

INSPECTOR 'Knacker of the Yard' Knacker today defended his award of a £1 million contract to his best friend.

Knacker had first met Mr Ronald McDodgy when they were on a skiing holiday in the Swiss resort of Grosse Scheister.

The two men immediately formed a strong bond, thanks to their shared interest in one of them getting a contract from the other.

It's A Blair Cop

When asked what services Mr McDodgy's firm had provided the Metropolitan Police, the Inspector said, "Considering there were large amounts of money involved, it would have been quite improper for me to know what services his company was offering.".

"All I know is that he was the best friend for the job."

'BUMBLING NERD' BROKE INTO PENTAGON AND CREATED HAVOC

by Our Defence Staff **Jim Hacker**

A MAN described as a "bumbling nerd" broke into the Pentagon and remained there for several years, leaving an astonishing trail of chaos behind him with a series of "juvenile and irresponsible pranks", ranging from an invasion of Iraq to an invasion of Iran.

The bespectacled lunatic was last night named as Don "Donny" Rumsfeld, 63, who claimed that he had hacked his way into the heart of the Pentagon only in the hope of discovering "intelligent life".

After meeting President Bush, he abandoned his quest, and began to vandalise (Cont. p. 94)

Knife crime at the highest level

Daily Mail

FRIDAY, AUGUST 22, 2008

FURY AT 'GUILTY' STAGG PAY-OUT

by Mail Crime Staff
Ben Schottgun

FURY erupted last night at the news that loner Colin Stagg, nearly found guilty of the murder of Rachel Nickell on Wimbledon Common is to receive compensation of £706,000.

Stagg, known to have a book about the occult and a number of dangerous knives, including a breadknife and the knife he used to butter his toast, was lucky to be freed as the result of a "legal blunder".

Gordon Honeytrap

Last night leading backbench Tory Simon Moffett expressed

Murderous weirdo

outrage when we contacted him at his holiday home in Crete.

"Why are you ringing me at eight o'clock in the morning?" he fumed. "I'm on holiday with my wife and kids."

LEADER, p.94.

WEDDING OF THE CENTURY

How They Are Related

Cherry Blossom Shoe Polish	Maxwell House Instant Coffee
Delmonte's Tinned Peaches	Robert Maxwell
Geldof the Wizard	Maxwell Hastings
Bob the Builder	Maxwell Gin Drummey
Honeysuckle Rose	Bulldog Drummy
Rosehip Syrup	Max Wall
Peaches W.B. Yates	**Rock Drummer**

BRITISH GAS 'PUTS PROFITS UP'

BRITISH GAS today defended its shock announcement that it would be putting profits up over the next twelve months by a whopping 35 percent.

"Obviously a company such as ours thinks long and hard about the effect on our bonuses before taking the decision to put profits up massively," said the chief executive of British Gas's parent company Centrica.

"But if we're to continue the board's massive investment programme in second homes in Provence and first-class holidays to the Caribbean then a rise in profits such as this is unavoidable."

British Gas refuses to rule out another massive wave of profit increases in 2009. *(Reuters)*

WESTON-SUPER-MARE'S PEER BURNT OUT

by Our Heritage Correspondent **Lynne National-Trust**

ONE of the nation's best-loved heritage items, Lord Archer of Weston-super-Mare, went up in smoke yesterday, in what was described as "a disaster for anyone who loves England".

The famous peer had given generations of holidaymakers hours of innocent fun with his long succession of best-selling books, which they read on the beach before leaving them behind in their hotel rooms.

Who could forget such legendary entertainments as *A Quiverful Of Lies, My Fragrant Wife* and *First Among Arseholes*?

Yet now he is no more than a twisted wreck, alone and abandoned on the foreshore, with nothing to remind him of the glory days when, by his own account, he was the first man to land on the moon, won a gold medal at the Berlin Olympics and rubbed shoulders with such political giants as Norman Fowler, John Selwyn Gummer and Peter Bottomley.

Friday, 22 August, 2008

'THE FATHER I NEVER KNEW'

Jemima Puddleduck Tells Her Unique Story

FOR the first time ever, heiress Jemima Puddleduck, formerly married to Imran Fox, has spoken of her controversial man-eating father Sir Jaws Goldfinger.

In an exclusive interview, she told Nursery Times staff reporter Enid Blyton, "Many people just think of my father as a greedy, man-eating shark, biting people's legs off without any sympathy for the victim.

"It may be true that he did savage lots of innocent Toy Towners, but he never lost sight of the fact that he was a shark. And his father had been a shark before him. The family tradition of tearing people's limbs off meant a lot to him.

"He felt it deeply when public opinion in Toy Town turned against him. In the end, he wanted no more to do with them and swam off to Mexico."

And what of Jemima herself? "I'm a lot like my father. You might call me a

Pictured with her father

free spirit. But I often feel that it's in me to bite someone's leg off. But it's difficult, being a duck."

"Isn't your campaign against excessive packaging a little excessive?"

ARE 'A' LEVEL ATTACKS NOW FAR TOO EASY?

by **Ivan O'Level**

EVERY year around this time, my editor phones me up asking for a 2,000 word-article bemoaning the fact that A-level results are getting better and better.

But as I cut and paste the current ridiculous pass-rate figures into the exact same article I wrote last year, I wonder: is it now far too easy to attack A-levels? Can almost anyone do it and get a piece published in the newspapers? Are the pieces all now meaningless? Certainly when I was at school it was much harder to earn a big fat cheque by *(cont. p94)*.

In Today's Eye2

LIVING

● **STAIRLIFT TO THE STARS**

Eye2's expert **Rosie Rusbridger** tests the new Stannah Speedster

GOING PLACES

● **THE UNDISCOVERED HULL**

Bevis Stoddy finds there's more to Hull than just a newly-promoted football team

HEALTH

● **BEETROOT**

Is it nature's answer to sciatica? **Dr Stephen Thrush** on the trail of an overlooked vegetable that could alter the lives of millions of sciatica sufferers

LIFESTYLE

● **YAK YAK**

Former hedge-fund dynamo **Derek Prune** and his partner ex-PR **Dotti Mckay** followed the trail to Nepal. Now they produce authentic yoghurt made from yak's milk – and it's now available in Harrods!

COLLECTING

● **BAG IT!**

Think twice before you throw away that plastic shopping bag. **Hugo Hughes-Onslow** last month saw an M&S bag from 1987 fetch £1500 at Sotheby's.

All in Eye2
It's Where It's At!

Letters *to the Editor*

The Olympic Handover

SIR – Along I feel sure with your readers, I watched with horror the embarrassing spectacle of the so-called "handover" ceremony to London from Beijing (or Rangoon, as those of us who have been out east would still prefer to call it). Have we nothing better to show the world as a symbol of British achievement than a double-decker bus on which cavorted the yobbish Mr Beckham kicking a football and a half-naked popular female singer (whose name mercifully escapes me), accompanied on the electric guitar by a German gentleman whose only claim to fame was to have invented the Zeppelin airship? Why on earth could we not have staged a pageant more in keeping with our country's contribution to world history and culture? Where, I should like to know, were the band of the Coldstream Guards? Where was the fly-past of Spitfires, Hurricanes and Sopwith Camels? Where were the serried ranks of Boy Scouts, Girl Guides and members of the Women's Institute? Where were our Morris dancers, the envy of the world? Where were London's proud traffic wardens with their gaily-coloured uniforms? Where were our celebrated "promenaders" waving their Union Jacks as they sang Land of Hope and Glory? And where, above all, was Her Majesty the Queen surrounded by her beloved Corgis, a supreme symbol of Britain's sporting achievement down the ages? No wonder that we all turned off our televisions off in sorrow and in shame. How ill this spectacles bodes for the kind of national humiliation we can expect when London plays host to the world in 2012.

Sir Herbert Gussett
The Old Velodrome, Addlington, Cheshire.

SIR – Half an hour after one Chinese Olympic Games, I find that I want another one!
Mike Giggler
Via email.

The Guardian   Friday September 5 2008

Letters and emails

The Olympic Handover

Dear Sir,
Along I feel sure with all your readers, I felt totally and utterly sickened by the so-called "handover" ceremony to London from Beijing. Have we nothing better to show the world as a symbol of Britain's vibrant and pluralist multi-cultural society than the sight of the Tory buffoon Boris Johnson parading across the world stage as the epitome of effete and outmoded elitism? Where were the reggae bands and rap singers who have made the Notting Hill Carnival the envy of the world? Where were London's celebrated gay policemen marching with their truncheons proudly held high, for their rights to marry each other? Where were our world-famous wheelie-bin inspectors, quite rightly handing out penalties for overfull bins? And where, above all, was the supreme symbol of all that modern London stands for, Mr Ken Livingstone, surrounded by his treasured newts? No wonder we all turned off our televisions in sorrow and shame. What a sad contrast to the two-week long astonishing display of Socialist unity and achievement to which the world had just been treated by the People's Republic of China.
Yours faithfully,
Barry Spartfield
Parks and Events Director, Haringey Leisure Services Division (part of the Haringey Council Family – "Haringey, Working For You"

Dear Sir,
Will Chinese restaurants now be offering "Bird's Nest Stadium Soup"? It certainly looked good enough to eat!?!
Mike Giggler
Via email.

Are Olympics getting easier?

by Our Education Staff **A.A.A. Gill**

AS THIS year's Olympic league tables were published showing a record number of gold, silver and bronze medals, the question is once again being asked "Are the Olympics just too easy?"

"It's ridiculous" said one expert, "In the old days you had to run really fast to get a medal. Nowadays you can just hop on a bike or climb on a boat. Don't tell me that standards haven't fallen (contd. p. 94)

"I wonder why we're so good at the sitting down events?"

The Youth of Britain
An Apology

IN COMMON with other papers, we may have given the impression in recent reports that we regarded the nation's youth as obese, lazy and obsessed with binge-drinking.

Headlines such as "Our Fat Kids Can't Even Walk" and "The On The Binge 24/7 Girls" may have led readers to conclude that the nation's youth was in a state of crisis and that we were breeding a generation of drink-sodden no hopers.

In the light of recent events in Beijing, we are happy to accept that there was not a jot or scintilla of truth in any of the above articles.

Headlines such as "Britain's Golden Girls and Boys" and "Super-Fit Brits Beat the World" will go some way, we trust, to reassure readers that our earlier reports were ill-founded and inappropriate.

We apologise unreservably for any offence we may have caused.

© All newspapers

AS A LOCAL RESIDENT OF BEIJING, WHAT HAS THE OLYMPICS MEANT TO YOU?

MY HOUSE!

My Beijing Diary

*by Boris Beano,
Mayor of London*

● Cripes! China is incredibly big and it's got a lot of chaps in it. Millions of them. Lots of them riding bikes like me. And they're all smiling away like billy-o, because they're all so jolly happy.

I know a lot of the sour grapes brigade go on about what a raw deal Johnny Chink gets, human rights and all that PC baloney. But once you've actually been there, like yours truly, you can see just how wrong they are. I mean, did you watch the Olympics opening bunfight, with all those millions of dancers banging drums and having the time of their lives? Happy as sandboys, every one of them. And what about those girls? Phwoar! Eh? It wasn't just the heat that made BoJo sweat under the old Eton collar, I can tell you! Golly!

● *Don't believe the knockers when they have a go at our brilliant London show, with the bus and chummy Becks kicking that football. I tell you, it was the highlight of the*

whole bally Games. And all the Chinese chappies were laughing away, saying that they'd never seen anything like it.

Sorry to swank, but the best moment of all was when they gave me the flag to wave about. "Be careful not to drop it," said my friend Mr Hu Hee. "We don't want you making a fool of yourself." I told him there was no chance of that. He then told me that if I did drop it I would be arrested and sent for twenty years' re-education in a distant province. Who says the Chinese don't have a sense of humour?

● Here's something else I bet you didn't know. You can't actually see the Great Wall of China from outer space. That's just one of those urban piffle things, like the Tibetan stuff.

No, according to my hosts, apparently the only thing you can see from space is Boris waving his flag!!! Beat that if you can, Dave Cameron! Oops! Better go now before I put my foot in it!!

POST-OLYMPIC EVENTS

HURDLES

HIGH JUMP

PARALLEL BARS

TRIUMPHANT HOMECOMING FOR BRITAIN'S GOLDEN PAEDOPHILE

THOUSANDS of hacks lined the streets yesterday to welcome home Britain's top paedophile Gary Glitter as he flew in from the Far East after his record- **breaking three years in gaol.**

Looking glad to be home, Mr Glitter sped off to a hero's welcome at the local police station.

● *Full story and pics of bearded man hiding from camera pp8-15.*

The Sun Says

ALL right-thinking *Sun* readers are disgusted that the vile predator Gary Glitter can be allowed to walk free on the streets of Britain.

Just yesterday the sick pervert was spotted in a newsagent on the south coast openly leering over a sickening publication he had just purchased – one in which young girls, most of whom barely look 18, expose their breasts on page 3 for the salacious pleasure of older men.

How perverts like Gary Glitter can be openly allowed to buy copies of perverted filth is *(You're sacked. Rupert.)*

"So what's your secret, Steroidos?"

MODERN SEA SHANTIES

What shall we do with the coked-up sailor
What shall we do with the coked-up sailor
What shall we do with the coked-up sailor
Early in the morning?

Put him on duty, drug-patrolling
Put him on duty, drug-patrolling
Put him on duty, drug-patrolling
Early in the morning?

© *HMS Ironic, The Royal Navy, c/o The Very High Seas*

QUEEN ADMITS 'YES, I NEVER DID COKE'

by Our Showbiz Staff **Phil Nostril**

IN A sensational interview with HMQ magazine, Her Majesty The Queen candidly admits that she never snorted cocaine when she was young and didn't enjoy it a great deal.

The Queen also confessed that she had not suffered in her career from "being blonde and having large breasts".

On Other Pages
● 'Yes, I Took Cake,' says Dame Helen **94**

FEARS GROW FOR CAROL THATCHER – HAS SHE LOST HER MARBLES?

by Our Mental Health Staff **Al Zheimer** and **Dee Mentia**

FRIENDS of Carol Thatcher are said to be increasingly concerned about her mental state, as she enters her twilight years.

Formerly spry, vivacious and forceful, Miss Thatcher is now said to be in a sad state of decline, unable to talk about anything except her mother.

At a recent literary luncheon, where Carol was billed to talk about her special subjects – skiing in Verbier and eating insects on TV's *I'm A Celebrity, Get Me Out Of Here* – she instead horrified her audience by blurting out "Mummy's gaga, you know. She's out to lunch... as indeed am I. Can I have my cheque, please?"

Carol Thatcher is 94.

"Three for the price of two"

HAPPY, DARLING?

You've never had it so bad!

Some mistake surely?

We're all doomed!

Well *you* are...

You can't have the Chancellor undermining the Prime Minister

Er... er...

LATE NEWS

THREE MEN CHARGED WITH BROWN PLOT

ANTI-TERROR police have confirmed that three men have been detained over an alleged plot against Gordon

Brown after a number of addresses in central London were raided overnight.

(Reuters)

"Sorry, pal... I don't really go for ginger blokes"

BLACK BRITISH HISTORY NOW TOPS CURRICULUM

by Our Education Staff **Conrad Blackboard**

THE teaching of history in Britain's schools is to be given a new look, under guidelines drawn up by the Qualifications Advisory Curricular Knowledge Educational Reorganisation Service (QUACKERS).

Said the board's director, Mr Ray Pilchard, "Our aim is to reorient the learning experience away from a white monofocus towards a more diverse, multi-cultural awareness of the paramount contribution made by ethnic minorities to the formation of British identity over the centuries."

OUT GO

● **Winston Churchill**

● **William Shakespeare**

● **The Venerable Bede**

IN COME

● **Leroy Onanugu**, who was a stretcher-bearer at the Battle of Waterloo, and may well have turned the course of the battle, although no evidence has yet come to light to support this theory (1794-1847 – but don't worry, dates are no longer important!).

● **The Rev. Amos Marley**, a Jamaican clergyman who is credited with inventing the trouserpress a full two centuries before Mr Corby claimed credit for the device that has won him world fame (dates 1705-62 – though again these are not important and all candidates are to forget them at once).

● **Jemima Hendrix**, Bristol fish-seller who would have been the first black woman to swim the English Channel if she had been given the chance to learn how to swim (dates 1901-1945 – or much the same time that the Nazi Holocaust was at its height, about which pupils will have learned in Key Stages 1, 2, 4, 5 and 7).

TIGER SHOT BY PUTIN

by Our Man in Siberia **Hunter Davies**

THE Russian Prime Minister last night sent a clear message to tigers everywhere not to oppose his policies.

Mr Putin shot the tiger in question after a disagreement over Russia's regional expansion in the Caucusus.

The tiger was believed to have expressed doubts about the re-establishment of Russian hegemony in states formerly belonging to the old Soviet

Union, thus provoking the Russian leader to shoot him.

Full story and pix. Huntin', Fishin', Putin p.94.

THAT MILIBAND ULTIMATUM TO PUTIN IN FULL

by Our Global Affairs Staff **Georgia W. Bush**

THE WORLD was stunned last night when David Miliband issued a stern ultimatum to Russia's prime minister Vladimir Putin over his recent attempts to start World War 3.

In forcefully undiplomatic language, Britain's no-nonsense Foreign Secretary warned the Russian dictator that if he carried on behaving in the same way as he had been doing for the last three weeks over Georgia and Ukraine

there might well be consequences that Mr Putin would regret.

Mr Millipede went even further. Making his position crystal clear, he told Mr Putin that if Russia invaded Britain then the British government would have to give serious consideration to the option of refusing to buy any more gas from Russia, possibly.

● That world-shaking Millipede speech in full **23-38.**

Russia formally recognises the state of...

...Western weakness!

95

NOT BROWN'S YEAR

FIRM DENIAL

SPELLING IT OUT

STOP AND SEARCH

IRAQ STRATEGY

VISION OF FUTURE

POLL SHOCK

OIL CRISIS TALKS

ENDANGERED SPECIES

NHS AT 60